MICROSOFT® PROJECT 2000 FOR DUMMIES®
QUICK REFERENCE

by Nancy Stevenson

D1710512

IDG Books Worldwide, Inc.
An International Data Group Company

Foster City, CA ✦ Chicago, IL ✦ Indianapolis, IN ✦ New York, NY

Microsoft® Project 2000 For Dummies® Quick Reference

Published by
IDG Books Worldwide, Inc.
An International Data Group Company
919 E. Hillsdale Blvd.
Suite 400
Foster City, CA 94404
www.idgbooks.com (IDG Books Worldwide Web site)
www.dummies.com (Dummies Press Web site)

Library of Congress Catalog Card No.: 00-101152

ISBN: 0-7645-0717-6

Printed in the United States of America

10 9 8 7 6 5 4 3 2 1

1P/RU/QU/QQ/IN

Distributed in the United States by IDG Books Worldwide, Inc.

Distributed by CDG Books Canada Inc. for Canada; by Transworld Publishers Limited in the United Kingdom; by IDG Norge Books for Norway; by IDG Sweden Books for Sweden; by IDG Books Australia Publishing Corporation Pty. Ltd. for Australia and New Zealand; by TransQuest Publishers Pte Ltd. for Singapore, Malaysia, Thailand, Indonesia, and Hong Kong; by Gotop Information Inc. for Taiwan; by ICG Muse, Inc. for Japan; by Intersoft for South Africa; by Eyrolles for France; by International Thomson Publishing for Germany, Austria and Switzerland; by Distribuidora Cuspide for Argentina; by LR International for Brazil; by Galileo Libros for Chile; by Ediciones ZETA S.C.R. Ltda. for Peru; by WS Computer Publishing Corporation, Inc., for the Philippines; by Contemporanea de Ediciones for Venezuela; by Express Computer Distributors for the Caribbean and West Indies; by Micronesia Media Distributor, Inc. for Micronesia; by Chips Computadoras S.A. de C.V. for Mexico; by Editorial Norma de Panama S.A. for Panama; by American Bookshops for Finland.

For general information on IDG Books Worldwide's books in the U.S., please call our Consumer Customer Service department at 800-762-2974. For reseller information, including discounts and premium sales, please call our Reseller Customer Service department at 800-434-3422.

For information on where to purchase IDG Books Worldwide's books outside the U.S., please contact our International Sales department at 317-596-5530 or fax 317-572-4002.

For consumer information on foreign language translations, please contact our Customer Service department at 1-800-434-3422, fax 317-572-4002, or e-mail rights@idgbooks.com.

For information on licensing foreign or domestic rights, please phone +1-650-653-7098.

For sales inquiries and special prices for bulk quantities, please contact our Order Services department at 800-434-3422 or write to the address above.

For information on using IDG Books Worldwide's books in the classroom or for ordering examination copies, please contact our Educational Sales department at 800-434-2086 or fax 317-572-4005.

For press review copies, author interviews, or other publicity information, please contact our Public Relations department at 650-653-7000 or fax 650-653-7500.

For authorization to photocopy items for corporate, personal, or educational use, please contact Copyright Clearance Center, 222 Rosewood Drive, Danvers, MA 01923, or fax 978-750-4470.

is a registered trademark under exclusive license to IDG Books Worldwide, Inc. from International Data Group, Inc.

About the Author

Nancy Stevenson has authored more than a dozen books on topics ranging from motivating employees to various software products and online productivity. Nancy is coauthor of *Microsoft Project 98 Bible,* published by IDG Books Worldwide, Inc. Currently a full-time author and publishing-industry consultant, Nancy has held several key management positions in publishing and the software industry in the past. In her capacity in the software industry, she has trained hundreds of employees of Fortune 500 companies in computer project management. Nancy has also been a technical-writing instructor at Indiana University-Purdue University in Indianapolis (IUPUI).

Dedication

This one is dedicated to my newest friend, Dylan; my sweetest friend, Tess; and my dearest friend, Graham.

Acknowledgments

My thanks to everyone at IDG Books for the opportunity to work with them once again — they're pros! Special thanks to Andy Cummings, who brought me back into the fold; Laura Moss, my most able acquisitions editor who's on top of everything, all at the same time; Jeanne Criswell for her adroit project editing and endless patience; and Vickey L. Quinn, who was there when I started working with project management and still helps to keep me accurate.

ABOUT IDG BOOKS WORLDWIDE

Welcome to the world of IDG Books Worldwide.

IDG Books Worldwide, Inc., is a subsidiary of International Data Group, the world's largest publisher of computer-related information and the leading global provider of information services on information technology. IDG was founded more than 30 years ago by Patrick J. McGovern and now employs more than 9,000 people worldwide. IDG publishes more than 290 computer publications in over 75 countries. More than 90 million people read one or more IDG publications each month.

Launched in 1990, IDG Books Worldwide is today the #1 publisher of best-selling computer books in the United States. We are proud to have received eight awards from the Computer Press Association in recognition of editorial excellence and three from Computer Currents' First Annual Readers' Choice Awards. Our best-selling ...For Dummies® series has more than 50 million copies in print with translations in 31 languages. IDG Books Worldwide, through a joint venture with IDG's Hi-Tech Beijing, became the first U.S. publisher to publish a computer book in the People's Republic of China. In record time, IDG Books Worldwide has become the first choice for millions of readers around the world who want to learn how to better manage their businesses.

Our mission is simple: Every one of our books is designed to bring extra value and skill-building instructions to the reader. Our books are written by experts who understand and care about our readers. The knowledge base of our editorial staff comes from years of experience in publishing, education, and journalism — experience we use to produce books to carry us into the new millennium. In short, we care about books, so we attract the best people. We devote special attention to details such as audience, interior design, use of icons, and illustrations. And because we use an efficient process of authoring, editing, and desktop publishing our books electronically, we can spend more time ensuring superior content and less time on the technicalities of making books.

You can count on our commitment to deliver high-quality books at competitive prices on topics you want to read about. At IDG Books Worldwide, we continue in the IDG tradition of delivering quality for more than 30 years. You'll find no better book on a subject than one from IDG Books Worldwide.

John Kilcullen
Chairman and CEO
IDG Books Worldwide, Inc.

WINNER
*Eighth Annual
Computer Press
Awards 1992*

WINNER
*Ninth Annual
Computer Press
Awards 1993*

WINNER
*Tenth Annual
Computer Press
Awards 1994*

WINNER
*Eleventh Annual
Computer Press
Awards 1995*

Publisher's Acknowledgments

We're proud of this book; please register your comments through our IDG Books Worldwide Online Registration Form located at http://my2cents.dummies.com.

Some of the people who helped bring this book to market include the following:

Acquisitions, Editorial, and Media Development

Senior Project Editor: Jeanne S. Criswell

Acquisitions Editor: Laura Moss

Copy Editor: Pam Wilson-Wykes

Technical Editor: Vickey L. Quinn

Media Development Editor: Heather Heath Dismore

Editorial Manager: Rev Mengle

Editorial Assistant: Candace Nicholson

Production

Project Coordinator: E. Shawn Aylsworth

Layout and Graphics: Amy Adrian, Joseph Bucki, Angela F. Hunckler, Tracy K. Oliver, Brent Savage

Proofreaders: Laura Albert, Corey Bowen, John Greenough, Susan Sims, Toni Settle

Indexer: Sharon Duffy

Special Help

Brian Kramer, Kathie Schutte, Dwight Ramsey

General and Administrative

IDG Books Worldwide, Inc.: John Kilcullen, CEO

IDG Books Technology Publishing Group: Richard Swadley, Senior Vice President and Publisher; Walter Bruce III, Vice President and Associate Publisher; Joseph Wikert, Associate Publisher; Mary Bednarek, Branded Product Development Director; Mary Corder, Editorial Director; Barry Pruett, Publishing Manager; Michelle Baxter, Publishing Manager

IDG Books Consumer Publishing Group: Roland Elgey, Senior Vice President and Publisher; Kathleen A. Welton, Vice President and Publisher; Kevin Thornton, Acquisitions Manager; Kristin A. Cocks, Editorial Director

IDG Books Internet Publishing Group: Brenda McLaughlin, Senior Vice President and Publisher; Diane Graves Steele, Vice President and Associate Publisher; Sofia Marchant, Online Marketing Manager

IDG Books Production for Dummies Press: Debbie Stailey, Director of Production; Cindy L. Phipps, Manager of Project Coordination, Production Proofreading, and Indexing; Tony Augsburger, Manager of Prepress, Reprints, and Systems; Laura Carpenter, Production Control Manager; Shelley Lea, Supervisor of Graphics and Design; Debbie J. Gates, Production Systems Specialist; Robert Springer, Supervisor of Proofreading; Kathie Schutte, Production Supervisor

Dummies Packaging and Book Design: Patty Page, Manager, Promotions Marketing

♦

The publisher would like to give special thanks to Patrick J. McGovern, without whom this book would not have been possible.

♦

Contents at a Glance

Table of Contents

Part XII: Reporting and Printing 153

Part XIII: Working Online with Microsoft Project 171

Appendix: Installation Requirements for Project Central 183

Glossary: Tech Talk 189

Index 195

Book Registration Information ......Back of Book

Microsoft Project 2000

Microsoft Project 2000 is the most popular project management software in the world today. Project management software helps you organize information about the timing of tasks, the costs incurred, and the project's resources (both the people and the materials) so that you stay on time and within budget and achieve your goals.

In this part . . .

What You See: The Gantt Chart View

Microsoft Project shows you information about your project in both graphics and text in various views, such as the Gantt Chart view shown here. For more information on what you can do with each of the features pointed out in this figure, check out the recommended section later in this book.

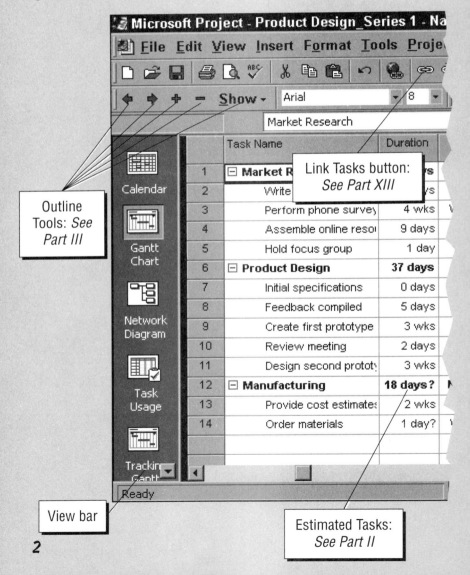

Outline Tools: *See Part III*

Link Tasks button: *See Part XIII*

View bar

Estimated Tasks: *See Part II*

2

Assign Resources
button: *See Part VII*

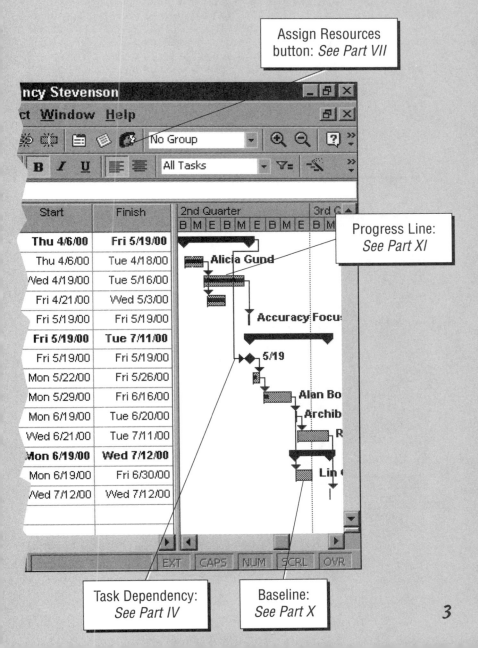

Progress Line:
See Part XI

Task Dependency:
See Part IV

Baseline:
See Part X

What You See: Dialog Boxes

You use dialog boxes in Microsoft Project to enter information about tasks, resources, the formatting of text and objects in a project plan, and so on. Dialog boxes — a familiar feature to Microsoft Windows users — typically have different tabs that logically divide the categories of information you can control. Dialog boxes appear when you make menu selections, click certain tools, or double-click cells within columns, such as the Task and Resource columns, of Microsoft Project views. The figure shows a typical Project dialog box.

 If a field name in a dialog box shows an underlined letter, such as Properties, press the Alt key plus that letter and your cursor will jump to that field. This underlining shortcut feature is also available for menu-command choices.

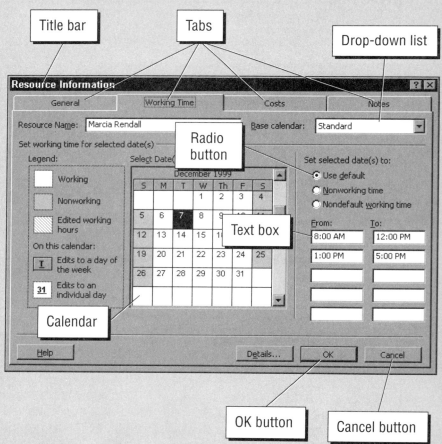

Title bar   Tabs   Drop-down list

Radio button

Text box

Calendar

OK button   Cancel button

✔ **Buttons:** Enable you to access Help, accept changes, close a dialog box without accepting changes, and so forth. Buttons ending with an ellipsis, such as Details..., indicate that another dialog box appears if you click that button, leading you to additional information.

✔ **Calendar:** Often appears in dialog boxes so that you can manage time and date settings.

✔ **Check box (not shown):** Turns one or more settings on or off when you click to add or remove a check mark.

✔ **Drop-down list:** Reveals a list of options when you click the downward-pointing arrow on the right side of a rectangle.

✔ **List box (not shown):** Functions similarly to a drop-down list, except that all the options are automatically displayed when the dialog box appears.

✔ **Radio button:** Appears as one of a series of options from which you select only one by clicking to place a small black dot inside the button.

✔ **Spinner (not shown):** Appears as a small box with a numeric setting that you can increase or decrease by clicking the up or down arrow beside the box.

✔ **Tab:** Appears as an index-card divider that you can click to display a page of information in a dialog box.

✔ **Text box:** Enables you to enter text, which can be any combination of numbers or letters.

✔ **Title bar:** Appears across the top of every dialog box and displays the dialog box's name.

Toolbar Table

The fastest way to get something done in Microsoft Project is by using tools. Tools are little buttons on toolbars that you can display on-screen for easy access. By default, Microsoft Project displays the Standard and Formatting toolbars. The Standard toolbar contains tools that initiate the tasks you commonly perform, such as creating a new task, cutting and pasting text or objects, and saving a file.

Tool/Button	Tool Name	What You Can Do	Shortcut	See
	New Document	Opens a blank Project file	Ctrl+N	The Big Picture
	Open	Opens an existing file	Ctrl+O	The Big Picture
	Save	Saves a file	Ctrl+S	The Big Picture
	Print	Prints a document	Ctrl+P	Part XII
	Print Preview	Displays a preview of a document	n/a	Part XII
	Spelling	Initiates spell checking	F7	Part IX
	Cut	Cuts selected text and holds it on the Clipboard	Ctrl+X	Part III
	Copy	Copies selected text and holds it on the Clipboard	Ctrl+C	Part III
	Paste	Pastes the Clipboard contents into a document	Ctrl+V	Part III
	Undo	Undoes the last action	Ctrl+Z	Part III
	Insert Hyperlink	Inserts a hyperlink to another document or Web page	Ctrl+K	Part XIII
	Link Tasks	Establishes a Finish-to-Start Dependency	Ctrl+F2	Part IV

Tool/Button	Tool Name	What You Can Do	Shortcut	See
⚡	Unlink Tasks	Unlinks two tasks	n/a	Part IV
⬚	Split Task	Splits task timing into two segments	n/a	Part II
☰	Task Information	Displays the Task Information dialog box	Shift+F2	Part II
✎	Task Notes	Displays the Notes tab of Task Information dialog box	n/a	Part II
👥	Assign Resources	Opens the Assign Resources dialog box	Alt+F10	Part VII
	Group By	Groups tasks by various criteria	n/a	Part VIII
🔍	Zoom In	Enlarges the display	n/a	The Big Picture
🔍	Zoom Out	Reduces the display	n/a	The Big Picture
?	Microsoft Project Help	Displays the Office Assistant	F1	The Big Picture

The side menu that appears when you make changes from the toolbar itself doesn't offer every possible tool, only the tools that Project associates with that type of toolbar. If you want to customize your toolbar to see all the tools, choose View➪ Toolbar➪Customize on the menu bar.

The Basics: Displaying Views

A project has many elements that a project manager may want to review, such as tasks to perform, completed tasks, resource allocations, accrued costs, work progress, and so on. Sometimes you may want to focus on one or more sets of information, which is why Microsoft Project views are so important.

 You can also use a view to generate a corresponding printout of your project that contains the information in that view.

To display a view in Microsoft Project, click in the View bar the icon for the view you want. (For more view options, scroll to the bottom of the View bar and click the More Views icon.) **See also** Part IX for more information about views and how to customize them.

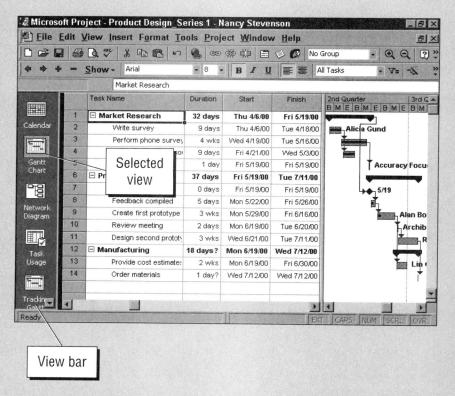

View bar

The Basics: Navigating around Project

In Microsoft Project, the main way to move around is to display different views and then use the scroll bars to move within those views. However, several views in Project display more than one *pane*. The Gantt View and the Tracking Gantt each have a spreadsheet section on the left with columns of information and a chart pane on the right graphically showing task timing by displaying taskbars.

You can use the Zoom In and Zoom Out tool buttons on the Standard toolbar to enlarge or reduce the display respectively.

Whether a view has a single pane or multiple panes, you can move within panes to view additional information by using the scroll bars. Scroll bars work in one of three ways:

- Clicking the arrows at either end of the scroll bar moves you up or down (if a vertical scroll bar) or from side to side (if a horizontal scroll bar).

- Clicking just below or just above the box in the scroll bar moves you half a page at a time.

- Clicking and dragging the box in the scroll bar quickly moves you through several pages, and an information box identifies the page location should you decide to release the mouse button at that point.

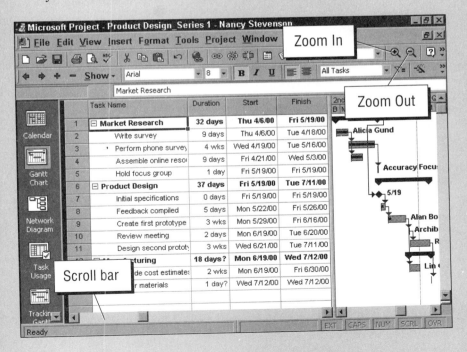

The Basics: Getting Help

Project has a standard Microsoft help system, including the Office Assistant (which you may be familiar with from other Microsoft Office products), online help, and the Contents and Index Help window (which contains Contents, Answer Wizard, and Index tabs). When you first start Project, the Contents and Index Help window appears with a blank project. You can also get to all the Help choices by choosing commands from the Help menu.

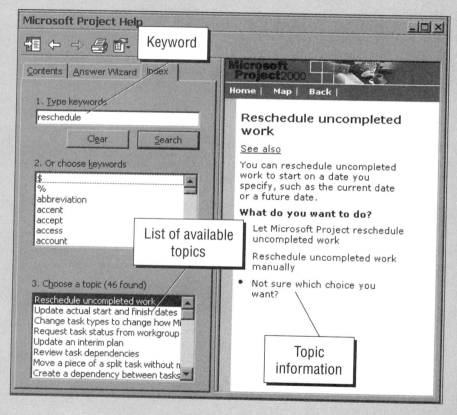

To open the Office Assistant, follow these steps:

1. Choose Help⇨Microsoft Project Help from the menu bar or click the Microsoft Project Help tool. The Office Assistant appears.

2. Click "Type Your Question Here" and then type your question.

3. Click the Search button. A list of possible topics to answer your question appears.

4. Click the topic you want, and an explanation appears.

To use the Help window, choose Help⇨Contents and Index from the menu bar. The following tabs appear:

- ✔ **Contents:** Gives you a Help table of contents. Click one item in each of the succeedingly more-detailed lists of topics to move from general to more-specific categories of information. Contents may work best if you're unsure of the proper terminology to use but know the general topic.

- ✔ **Answer Wizard (an English language interface):** Means you can type your question in simple English rather than sorting through layers of topics or using a keyword. Answer Wizard works in a similar fashion to the Office Assistant, without that annoying little character!

- ✔ **Index:** Enables you to search by specific words or phrases by using a keyword and then choosing from a topic list. Use Index if you know the exact term for the item you need help with.

After you find the answer you need in any of the Help areas, you can print the explanation by clicking the print icon or close the Help window by clicking the close button in the top right corner.

If you're connected to the Internet, you may want to use the Microsoft online help, which allows you to ask Microsoft your questions or to search through frequently asked questions that go beyond Project's built-in help system. To access online help, choose Help⇨Office on the Web.

If you're new to Microsoft Project, you may want to take advantage of the Getting Started item on the Help menu. Getting Started leads you to a tutorial to help you get acquainted with Project basics, a Project Map that gives you an overview of the lifecycle of a typical project, and a Quick Preview that demonstrates the main features of Project.

The Basics: Starting Project

As soon as you start Microsoft Project, a new file appears in the Gantt Chart view with the Help window displayed by default on top of the blank project. Follow these steps to start Project:

1. From the Windows Desktop, choose Start⇨Programs⇨Microsoft Project.

2. Click the Close button to close the Help window and reveal the Project screen.

The Basics: Opening a New File

If Project is running, you can open a blank new document file or a template (a file with preset tasks and other information already entered) by choosing File⇨New from the menu bar. The New dialog box appears with tabs labeled General, Project Templates, and Office Templates. You can then select one of the following options:

✔ **To open a blank document**, select the General tab, select Blank Document, and then click Open.

✔ **To open a template**, select either the Project Templates tab or the Office Templates tab, select the template you want, and then click Open.

The Basics: Opening an Existing File

To open an existing file, Project must be running, and you must know the file's location on your computer. Follow these steps to open an existing file:

1. Select File⇨Open from the menu bar. The Open dialog box appears.

2. Locate the file you want by using the Up One Level button or the drop-down list of files and folders.

3. Click to select the file and then click Open.

The Basics: Saving a Project File and Exiting

To avoid losing your work, you must save your Project file frequently. The first time you need to save a file, follow these steps:

1. With your file open, choose File⇨Save As. The Save As dialog box appears.

2. Use the Up One Level button to find the location on your hard drive or floppy disk where you want to save the file.

3. Type the filename in the File Name text box. Leave the Project file format in the Save As Type list box. Doing this saves the file as a Project file rather than in some alternate software format.

4. Click Save.

5. To exit Project, choose File⇨Exit.

After you save the file the first time, you can subsequently save it with the same name and file format by simply clicking the Save button on the Standard toolbar.

The Basics: Project Lifecycle

A project can last a few weeks or take years to complete. A project may involve you, three other people, and two cartons of materials; or it may span multiple departments, companies, budgets, and phases. Whatever the nature of your project, Microsoft Project helps you manage the various phases of the project's lifecycle.

Creating tasks

You create tasks in Project by filling out a task-information form.

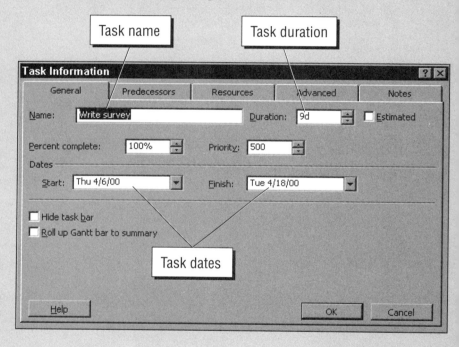

As you build your task list, you can organize your tasks by using Microsoft Project's outline structure for breaking sets of tasks into phases for a more logical structure. **See also** Part II for information on creating summary and subtasks in your project.

Assigning timing

In the Task Information dialog box, you enter a task's duration and beginning and ending dates. You can also enter task *constraints*, which are directions to Microsoft Project about task timing. After you set timing information, you can see a graphic representation of a task's length in the Gantt Chart view, which displays *taskbars* to show duration.

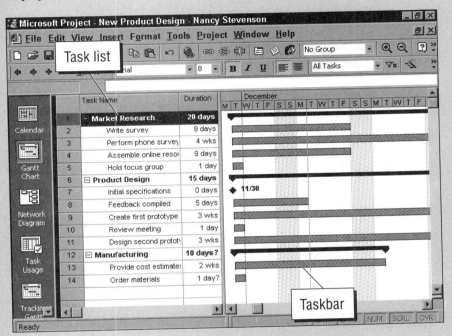

Establishing dependencies

You set task *dependency relationships* after you create your task list. Dependencies are constraints on the timing between tasks, such as a task that cannot start until another task is completed. In Project, the first task in a timing relationship is the *predecessor*, and the second is the *successor*. After you set dependencies (in the Predecessors tab of the Task Information dialog box), you can get a true idea of your project's overall timing. **See also** Part IV for information about setting dependency relationships.

Assigning resources

Resources can be people, groups of people, equipment, or materials and are categorized either as *work resources* or *material resources*. To create resources, you enter information in a resource sheet, setting specific parameters, such as a calendar that determines work-time availability. Resources also typically come at a cost, which is usually an hourly rate or a flat fee.

You assign resources to individual tasks and designate how many hours the resources are to spend working on each task. After the project is finished, you need to evaluate resource workloads and address any *resource conflicts,* such as a resource being used on too many tasks at a time or working excessive hours on any given day. Microsoft Project has several sophisticated tools to help you resolve any resource conflicts. **See also** Part VIII for information about solving resource conflicts.

Tracking progress

After you work out any timing kinks for tasks and resource assignments, you can set a *baseline* — a snapshot of your original project plan that's useful in tracking project activity. In Project, you record all the work put in by resources and all the costs for material resources. The hours and costs you log enable Project to add up total costs for your project.

Making adjustments

Comparing your original plan to any recorded activity lets you see if you're getting off track, so you can make adjustments. Microsoft Project provides several ways for you to get a picture of your original plan, including progress lines that appear on-screen alongside the baseline data. **See also** Part XI for more about tracking activity on your project.

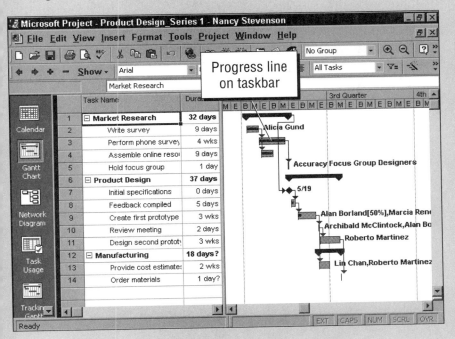

Reporting

As you move forward on a project, you'll appreciate the ability to generate sophisticated reports that let you see your progress from various perspectives. Microsoft Project contains impressive reporting features that enable you to report your progress quickly and easily to your management, project team members, or customers. **See also** Part XII to find out about formatting and generating a wide variety of reports.

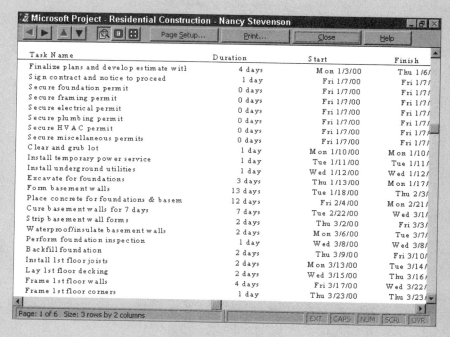

What You Can Do: Track Project Progress

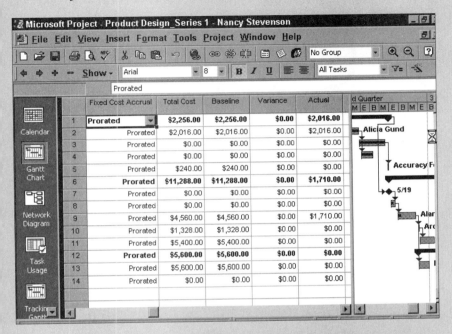

Microsoft Project's greatest strength is the wealth of information it provides for tracking your project's progress. You can display dozens of columns of information showing variances from your original estimates and even see those variances represented graphically in several Project views. To track your project's progress, you can

1. Get started by

Building and Organizing Tasks, Part II
Refining and Finalizing Your Project Plan, Part VIII
Saving Your Baseline and Protecting Your Project, Part X

2. Work on your project by

Monitoring Project Activity, Part XI
Recording Resource Effort, Part XI
Reporting Progress, Part XII

3. Add finishing touches by

Interacting with Workgroups Online, Part XIII
Printing Reports, Part XII
Communicating with Workgroups, Part XIII

What You Can Do: Manage Resource Allocation

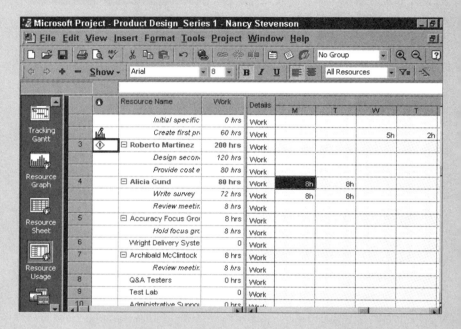

In life, time is money. In Microsoft Project, resource-time is money. When you create resources, allocate their costs, and track the time those resources work on a project, you can see what you're spending. Project provides some very helpful tools for wisely managing the time of those resources. To manage resource allocation, you can

1. **Get started by**

   Defining Resources, Part V

   Associating Resources with Costs, Part VI

   Making Resource Assignments, Part VII

2. **Work on your project by**

   Monitoring Resource Workload, Part VIII

   Reducing Total Time, Part VIII

   Recording Resource Effort, Part XI

3. **Add finishing touches by**

   Updating Project Data with Project Central, Part XIII

   Tracking Work with Microsoft Outlook, Part XIII

   Entering Resources in the Outlook Address Book, Part XIII

What You Can Do: Get Online with Project Central

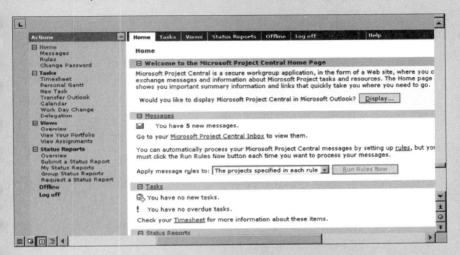

New to Microsoft Project 2000 is Project Central, companion software that Microsoft includes with Project 2000. Project Central lets people in a workgroup interact online. Using Project Central, project team members who don't actually have Microsoft Project installed can view, work on, and communicate over the Internet about a project's schedule. To get online with Project Central, you can

1. Get started by

Installing and Configuring Project Central, Appendix

Sharing Resources Across Projects, Parts V and XIII

Adding Hyperlinks, Part XIII

2. Work on your project by

Tracking Progress, Part XI

Tracking Resource Time Spent on a Project, Part XI

Automating Resource Reporting, Part XI

3. Add finishing touches by

Communicating with Workgroups, Part XIII

Linking Tasks to Other Projects, Part XIII

Sharing Work Online, Part XIII

Creating Your Project Plan

Okay, you're ready to start your project. You have a million details about resources, tasks, dates, and so on. But before you begin working with all those details, you need to enter some general project information and make some basic settings in your Microsoft Project 2000 file. For example, you can name the project, specify the project manager, enter the start or finish date for the entire project, and set the project calendar. This part shows you how to make these basic settings for your overall project, creating the framework for all the details you add later.

In this part . . .

Creating Custom Properties

Project provides several fields in the Properties dialog box, such as the project name and the start and finish dates. However, you may want to add other general project information, such as the department that's driving the project or the client for whom the work is being done. To add such information, you create a custom property field by following these steps:

1. Choose File⇔Properties from the menu bar. The Properties dialog box appears.

2. Click the Custom tab.

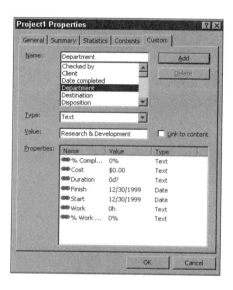

3. In the Name list box, click a property to select it. Use the scroll bar to see additional properties, if necessary.

4. In the Type drop-down list box, select the type of information — Text, Number, Date, or Yes/No — to appear in the field.

5. In the Value text box, type a value for the field. For example, if you choose Department in the Name text box, type the department's name in the Value text box. If you want to link the custom property to the contents of another field in the file, click to put a check mark in the Link to Content check box.

6. Click Add, and the custom property appears in the Properties list at the bottom of the dialog box.

7. Click OK to close the dialog box.

Entering project properties

When you begin a new project, you probably want to enter some general information about that project, such as its title, the author of the project file, and the project manager. You may also want to enter some keywords by which you can search for the file at a later date, or a path to a file where you keep supporting documents. You can do this by using the Summary tab in the Properties dialog box.

 You can't edit some fields in the Properties dialog box because Project inserts the fields automatically from entries you make in other locations, such as the Project Information dialog box.

To enter your project's general parameters, follow these steps:

1. Choose File⇨Properties from the menu bar. The Properties dialog box appears.

2. Click the Summary tab.

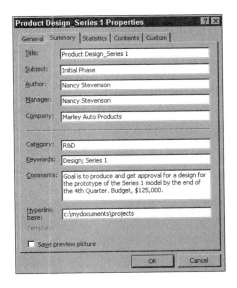

3. Enter information in any of the fields.

4. If you want to save a preview of this file, click to put a check mark in the Save Preview Picture check box. A preview image of the file is then displayed in the Open File dialog box whenever you open the file.

5. Click OK.

If you do decide to save a preview of the file, be aware that doing so adds to your file's size because you're adding a graphic element.

Linking to supporting documents

The first step in creating links to documents that are relevant to your Project file is to enter hyperlink base information. This information provides the path to a folder where you store most of the documents you want to link to. If you enter this hyperlink base information in the file properties, you don't have to enter that path information over and over again every time you insert a link at the task level.

To enter hyperlink base information, follow these steps:

1. Choose File➪Properties from the menu bar. The Properties dialog box appears.

2. Click the Summary tab in the Properties dialog box.

3. Type the path in the Hyperlink Base text box.

4. Click OK.

To establish a link from a task in your project to a document or Web page, follow these steps:

1. Click the task name in the Gantt Chart or other view to select it. You can select which view to display from the View bar along the left side of the Project screen.

2. Choose Insert➪Hyperlink. The Insert Hyperlink dialog box appears.

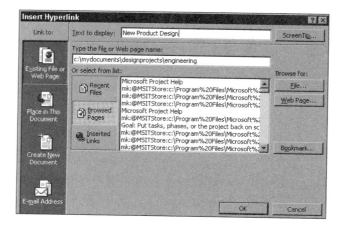

3. Enter the path for the file in the Type the File or Web Page Name text box.

4. If you don't know the path to the linked document, use the buttons under the Or Select from List and Browse For areas to search for the document.

5. Click OK.

In various views, a symbol appears next to the task, indicating that the task contains a link. By clicking the symbol, you can open the document or Web page that the task links to.

If you want Project to display information whenever a pointer rests on the hyperlink symbol, enter a title for the link in the Text to Display field of the Insert Hyperlink dialog box. You can also click the ScreenTip button in that same dialog box to add a note about the link that will appear under the title whenever a pointer rests on the hyperlink symbol.

Setting general project timing

When you begin a project, you probably have some idea about when you plan to begin working and what your desired completion date is. You can give your project some general timing parameters by entering them in the Project Information dialog box:

1. Choose Project⇨Project Information from the menu bar. The Project Information dialog box appears.

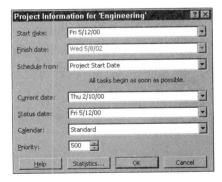

2. Click the arrow to the right of the Start Date field. A calendar appears.

3. Click to select the date when you want the project to start. If you need to go to a month other than the current one, use the calendar's right or left arrows to move forward or backward one month at a time.

4. Click OK.

After you choose the start date, the finish date appears automatically, based on the tasks you previously entered and their associated durations and dependency relationships.

If you must meet a specific completion date, and you prefer to plan your project backward from that date, select Project Finish Date in the Schedule From drop-down list box and enter an end date. Project calculates the start date for you.

Viewing Project Statistics

At any point in your project, you can get an overview of the project's start and finish dates, duration, costs, and so forth, by viewing Project Statistics. Doing so gives you a great overview of where you stand at the moment in relation to your original plan. You can display these and other statistics by following these steps:

1. Choose Project⇨Project Information from the menu bar. The Project Information dialog box appears.

2. Click the Statistics button. The Project Statistics dialog box appears.

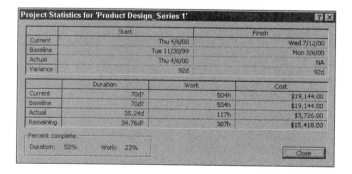

The Project Statistics dialog box displays the following information:

- **Current:** Shows the Start and Finish dates based on any tracked progress on individual tasks and any baseline tasks that still need to be done.

- **Baseline:** Shows the Start and Finish dates according to the last saved baseline.

- **Actual:** Shows the Start and Finish dates for work done to date.

- **Variance:** Shows how many project days you've varied from your baseline estimate.

- **Current:** Under Duration/Work/Cost, shows the length of the project, hours of work performed, and costs accrued, based on any actual progress tracked plus any remaining baseline work.

- **Baseline:** Under Duration/Work/Cost, shows the data in the Current row according to the last saved baseline.

- **Actual:** Under Duration/Work/Cost, shows this information only for actual work performed to date.

- **Remaining:** Under Duration/Work/Cost, shows how much schedule time, hours of effort, and budgeted money remains.

- **Percent Complete:** Indicates the percentage of time and effort previously estimated for the project that's complete as of the current date.

3. Click Close after you finish reviewing the information.

See also Part XI for more information on ways to view project status while tracking activity.

 For more about tracking costs and work performed, see *Microsoft Project 2000 For Dummies,* by Martin Doucette, published by IDG Books Worldwide, Inc.

Setting File Attributes

You can set certain file attributes for your project. These attributes help to keep your file safe, because they control how people can access your file and whether Windows performs backups of your file. To set file attributes, choose from these options:

✔ **Read only:** Designates a file that can be viewed but not changed. This option protects the information in the file so that others using the file can't accidentally (or not-so-accidentally) change or delete the file.

✔ **Archive:** Designates a file to be backed up.

✔ **Hidden:** Designates a file that can't be seen when browsing your system. You have to know the file's name to open it.

✔ **System:** Designates a file that the operating system requires. System files must always be functional for Windows to work. (You aren't likely to need this setting for a Project file.)

To changes file attributes, follow these steps:

1. From the Windows desktop, choose Start⇔Programs⇔Windows Explorer. Windows Explorer opens.

2. Right-click the filename for the project you want to change. A shortcut menu appears.

3. Select Properties from the shortcut menu. The Properties dialog box appears.

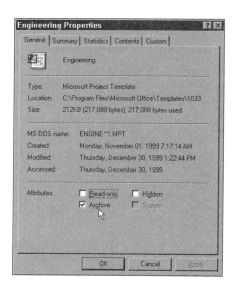

4. Click the check box for any attribute — Read-Only, Archive, and Hidden — you want to activate. You can use these attributes singly or in combination by checking as many of them as you need.

5. Click OK.

Your attributes for the file are set. You can change them at any time by following the same steps.

Setting Up the Working Calendar

Calendars are an important part of Project. You can set calendars for individual resources and tasks, but your first step is to set the general project calendar. You can also designate specific days of the year as nonworking days, or set a nondefault working time for any day you want. *See also* Part V for more information on resource calendars.

Get more details about how to use calendar settings in *Microsoft Project 2000 For Dummies,* by Martin Doucette, published by IDG Books Worldwide, Inc.

Setting up project working days

Setting the project calendar (also called the working calendar) establishes the workday that Project uses when you enter a duration for a task. The project calendar also establishes the default calendar for resources. In setting the overall project calendar, you can choose from Standard, 24 Hours, and Night Shift.

To set the project calendar, follow these steps:

1. Choose Project⇨Project Information from the menu bar. The Project Information dialog box appears.

2. Select the appropriate project calendar in the Calendar drop-down list.

    • **Standard:** Designates an eight-hour workday, from 8 a.m. to 5 p.m., with an hour lunch break at noon

    • **24 Hours:** Designates that work continues throughout the entire day

    • **Night Shift:** Designates that work goes on from midnight to 8 a.m., with an hour off from 3 a.m. to 4 a.m.

3. Click OK.

Setting nonworking days

You can change the working calendar to accommodate times when you know people won't be working. For example, if your company doesn't work on certain days, such as the week between Christmas and New Year's Day, you want to set this interval as nonworking time by following these steps:

1. Choose Tools⇨Change Working Time. The Change Working Time dialog box appears.

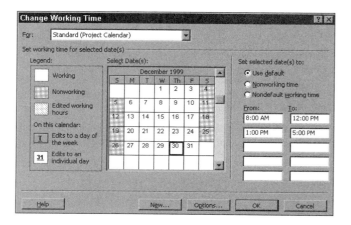

2. Locate the month in which you want to make a change by using the scroll bar on the right side of the calendar.

3. Click the days you want to make nonworking days.

4. Click to select the Nonworking Time radio button.

5. Click OK.

   The blocks representing any date you designated as nonworking time become shaded in the Change Working Time dialog box.

Setting nondefault working time

Suppose your company works half a day on the days before Christmas and Thanksgiving. You can adjust the working time for specific days in the project calendar by following these steps:

1. Choose Tools⇨Change Working Time. The Change Working Time dialog box appears.

2. Locate the month you want in the calendar and click the day you want to edit.

3. Click to select the Nondefault Working Time radio button.

4. Enter the start time in the first From text box and the finish time in the first To text box.

5. To indicate breaks in time, such as a lunch hour, enter From and To times in the subsequent sets of boxes that represent the various working portions of the day.

6. Click OK.

Now whenever you enter work on the date that you just modified in your project, work can only go on for the number of working hours you set for the day.

Part II

Building Tasks

The major building blocks for any project are the tasks you have to perform to reach your goal. Creating tasks is simple, but as you create a task, you have to think about some details — such as the length of the task, where the task fits in with the various phases of your project, and whether to break down one large task into smaller tasks. The good news is that after you create your to-do list, you have the framework for your project in place. This part gives you information about creating tasks and specifying their timing by using durations and task calendars.

In this part . . .

ng a Task Note

You may want to add information — such as phone numbers or important meeting reminders — to a specific task. You add such information in a task note. To enter information in a task note, follow these steps:

1. Choose Project➪Task Notes from the menu bar, or simply double-click a task name displayed in any view. The Task Information dialog box appears.

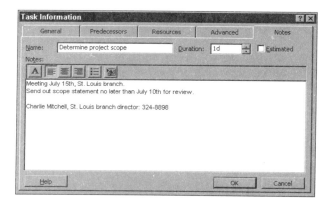

2. Type any notes you want in the space provided.

3. Use the formatting tools located above the text box to align selected text, change the font, or create a bulleted list.

4. Click OK.

 Discover more information about common text formatting features in *Microsoft Word 2000 For Dummies,* by Dan Gookin, published by IDG Books Worldwide, Inc.

 Tip: You can also insert an object, such as a graphic element, into a task note by clicking the Insert Object tool to the right of the formatting tools.

Creating a Recurring Task

If a project has a regularly occurring task — such as a quarterly inspection or a monthly executive review meeting — you don't have to create multiple tasks. You can save yourself effort by simply creating one recurring task by following these steps:

1. Choose Insert⇨Recurring Task from the menu bar. The Recurring Task Information dialog box appears.

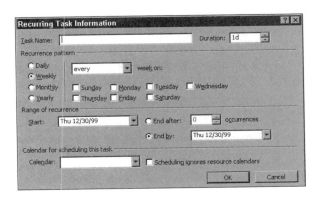

2. Enter a name in the Task Name text box.

3. Click to select the radio button for a Recurrence Pattern: Daily, Weekly, Monthly, or Yearly. Depending on your choice of pattern, you may need to make additional selections, such as what day the task falls on.

4. Select a start date from the Start drop-down calendar.

5. If you want the task to stop after a certain number of occurrences or on a specific date, click to select the respective radio button, and then type the information in the End After Occurrences or End By fields.

6. Click OK. The task appears in a Gantt Chart spreadsheet as one summary task with one duration but with multiple taskbars reflecting the designated timing for each occurrence spread across your schedule. To see the individual tasks and their timing, click the plus sign to open the summary task.

In the Recurring Task dialog box, you can also set the calendar on which the task is based. *See also* "Working with Task Calendars" later in this part.

Creating a Task

Think of a project task as an item on a long to-do list. You create a task for each step in your project, and then you attach certain information to that task, such as task duration and resources.

create a new task, perform the following steps:

1. Click the Gantt Chart icon in the View bar along the left side of the Project screen. The Gantt Chart view appears.

2. Click the task located just below where you want to insert the new task.

3. Choose Insert⇨New Task from the menu bar. A blank row appears above the task you selected.

4. Click the blank cell in the Task Name column and type a name for the task.

TIP

You can also insert new tasks when displaying other views. Doing this simply requires that you display a view, such as the Tracking Gantt or Network Diagram, that includes a column or graphic object representing each task. To display a view, click the View bar icon along the left side of the Project screen.

Designating Task Type

The timing of your tasks is key to an accurate project. First, you assign a duration, which is the length of time it takes to complete a task. Then you assign the resources who will work (also referred to as effort) on the task throughout its duration. Keep in mind that each resource may have different availability. For example, if a resource works only half days on a three-day assignment, that resource puts in 12 hours of work. Or, if three full-time resources are assigned to a three-day task, those resources will put in 24 hours of resource effort. So, the effort made by resources during the duration of the task is not equal to the length of the task.

Task types control what takes precedence in establishing task timing. Project enables you to designate three different task types, as follows:

✔ **Fixed Duration.** The amount of time required to complete the task remains the same, no matter the number of assigned resources. For example, a business presentation for which you're allotted one hour takes one hour, no matter how many people speak. The duration you enter is the controlling factor for task timing.

✔ **Fixed Units.** The resource percentages assigned to the task stay the same, even if the required work (number of resource hours needed to complete the task) changes. The duration you enter in combination with resource effort determines task timing.

✔ **Fixed Work.** The required work (number of resource hours to complete the task) rules the task timing. After you enter the duration of a task, Microsoft Project determines the effort required to complete the task in the time allotted each resource. Fixed-work tasks change duration based on the number of resources assigned to the tasks. With this task type, resource effort controls task timing.

To set a task type, follow these steps:

1. Click the Gantt Chart icon in the View bar along the left side of the Project screen. The Gantt Chart view appears.

2. Double-click a task name to display the Task Information dialog box.

3. Click the Advanced tab.

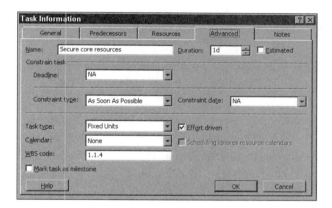

4. Select a task type from the Task Type drop-down list box.

5. Click OK.

Establishing Task Length

All tasks have their own unique timing. The length of a task can range from minutes to months. Some tasks, called milestones, are simply markers of a moment in time and as such don't have any duration at all. Regardless of the length of a task, a duration for each task needs to be specified.

Avoid creating tasks that have a lengthy duration, such as a year. A long duration gives you less flexibility to deal with schedule adjustments to accommodate inevitable delays (because you have no interim tasks that you can adjust). If a task is longer than a month or two, break down the task into subtasks.

Entering a task duration

You can enter a task duration by using either of these methods:

✔ Display the Task Information dialog box by choosing Project⇨Task Information from the menu bar and then enter a duration on the General tab.

✔ Display a spreadsheet view that contains a duration column (such as the Gantt Chart, Tracking Gantt, or Task Usage view) by clicking the corresponding icon in the View bar. Click the duration cell for a task and then either type or use the spinner arrows to set a duration in the cell.

If you have a long list of tasks and want to enter all the durations at one time, the spreadsheet method is definitely faster.

Marking a task duration as an estimate

In a sense, any time you set a task duration, you make an estimate based on your experience with similar tasks, or on information that project vendors or resources give you about how much time the task requires. Sometimes, however, you're in the dark about how long a task will take, but you still need to enter a duration. You want to alert your team and management that the duration may vary from the time you've assigned. So, you mark the duration as an estimate, which puts a question mark next to the duration wherever it appears in your schedule or reports.

To mark a task duration as an estimate, follow these steps:

1. Click the Gantt Chart icon in the View bar along the left side of the Project screen. The Gantt Chart view appears.

2. Double-click a task name to display the Task Information dialog box.

3. Click the Advanced tab.

4. Click to place a check mark in the Estimated check box.

5. Click OK.

If at some point you want to remove the estimated status from the task, simply repeat the steps above and then click the Estimated check box to remove the check mark.

Making tasks effort-driven

By default, Microsoft Project makes the timing of all tasks effort-driven. That means that as you change resource assignments, the task duration may change, but the work hours required to complete the task remain constant. With an effort-driven task, Project distributes the work equally among resources.

You can turn off the effort-driven setting. If you do, Project won't change the original work allocation for individual resources. With a non-effort-driven task, when you add or take away resources, the duration of the task doesn't adjust in any way.

To turn off the effort-driven feature, complete the following steps:

1. Click the Gantt Chart icon in the View bar along the left side of the Project screen. The Gantt Chart view appears.

2. Double-click a task name to display the Task Information dialog box.

3. Click the Advanced tab.

4. Click the Effort Driven check box to remove the check mark.

5. Click OK.

 If you select Fixed Work from the Task Type drop-down list, the effort-driven option isn't available to you. With the Fixed Work task type, any change to resource assignments has no impact on the work required to complete the task, and task duration is determined when the work has been completed. *See also* "Designating Task Type" earlier in this part for more information on task types and their effect on task duration.

Defining a task as a milestone

A milestone is a task that has no duration; it simply marks a moment in your schedule, such as the moment when you get a design approval. The symbol for a milestone on the Gantt Chart is a diamond with a date beside it — which makes milestones easy to spot on a schedule. To create a milestone, follow these steps:

1. Click the Gantt Chart icon in the View bar along the left side of the Project screen. The Gantt Chart view appears.

2. Type **0** in the task's Duration column.

Specifying a Split Task

Some tasks start, stop for a while, and then start again. When that happens, you can split a task into timing segments — which is especially useful if, for example, a task is put on hold temporarily because of budget constraints or lack of resources. To split a task's timing, follow these steps:

1. Click the Gantt Chart icon in the View bar along the left side of the Project screen. The Gantt Chart view appears.

2. Click a Task Name cell to select the task you want to split.

3. Click the Split Task button on the Formatting toolbar. A floating box appears attached to your cursor. As you move your cursor around the timescale portion (which is like a scrolling graphic calendar) of the Gantt Chart, information appears in this box indicating the timeline associated with where your cursor is placed. To make finding the right place to insert the split easier for you, as you move your cursor across the task, the floating box indicates the exact moment that is associated with the cursor position.

4. When the right date appears in the box, click the place in the taskbar where you want to insert a split, and then drag that portion of the taskbar that's to the right of your cursor to the place in the Gantt Chart where you want the task to start again. Watch the date display in the Split Task box to locate the correct new start date.

5. Release your mouse. The designated segment of the taskbar is placed at its new start date.

You can insert several splits into a single task. To rejoin a split task, simply drag and return the split segment of a taskbar to a previously adjoining segment. The two segments then reconnect.

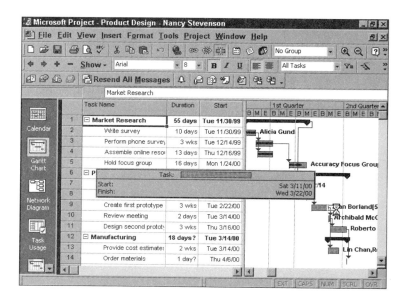

Summary Tasks and Subtasks

In the hierarchy of your project outline, you have two categories of tasks — summary tasks and subtasks. Each summary task summarizes the detail tasks, called subtasks, listed beneath it. A summary task has no timing of its own. Instead, its timing is the total timing of its subtasks, taking into account their timing relationships with other tasks. This hierarchy of summary and subtasks helps you open and close your project outline to view different levels of detail depending on your information needs.

To change a task into a subtask, you simply indent the task by following these steps:

1. Click the Gantt Chart icon in the View bar along the left side of the Project screen. The Gantt Chart view appears.

2. Choose a task.

3. Click the Indent button.

When you look at a schedule with summary tasks and subtasks, with their duration times assigned, you can see that summary tasks take their timing from the subtasks listed beneath them. The highest level of summary task is a summary of the entire project. Because summary tasks can occur at any level of the outline, you can create multiple levels of detail. *See also* Part III for more information on working with outlines.

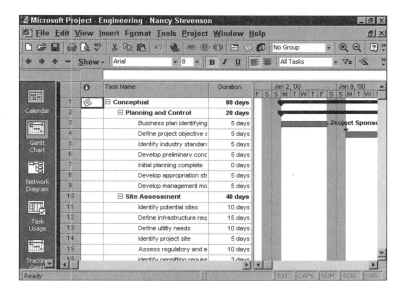

Working with Task Calendars

A feature that's new to Microsoft Project 2000 is the ability to set a task calendar. You set a task calendar if a particular task requires a calendar that's different from the working calendar for the entire project. You can choose from among three calendar options, which are Standard, 24 Hours, and Night Shift. To modify the calendar of an individual task, complete the following steps:

1. Click the Gantt Chart icon in the View bar along the left side of the Project screen. The Gantt Chart view appears.

2. Double-click the task name to display the Task Information dialog box.

3. Click the Advanced tab.

4. Click the arrow in the Calendar field to display a drop-down calendar.

5. Click the arrow to the right of the drop-down calendar to display the following three choices:

   - **Standard:** An eight-hour day, from 8:00 a.m. to 5:00 p.m.

   - **24 Hours:** A consecutive 24-hour day

   - **Night Shift:** An eight-hour shift, from midnight to 8:00 a.m.

6. Click the calendar you want to use.

7. Click OK.

See also Part I for more information on the working calendar for the entire project.

Part III

Outlining

A project's task list is actually a to-do list, and the outline feature helps you organize your tasks. Outlining lets you create task families and break up your project into manageable phases. Using an outline also helps you apply structure and sequence to your tasks and makes your project reports easier to follow. This part shows you how to create and manipulate an outline structure for your tasks in Microsoft Project 2000.

In this part . . .

Applying Outline Structures

You've probably worked with outlines before, using numbers or letters to indicate a project's tasks and to group the tasks into levels. In Project, an outline structure basically reflects the different task levels in your project. In a large project, with perhaps hundreds of tasks, outline codes uniquely help each task.

In Project, you can use a variety of coding schemes to designate an outline's task levels. A standard outline code that's built into Project is called WBS (work breakdown structure). The government and other large organizations often use WBS codes as a way of standardizing reports. Using Project, you can also easily create your own custom-coding structures.

Working with WBS codes

WBS is a simple coding scheme that uses numbers or letters to reflect an outline's task levels. For example, a project using a WBS numerical coding system looks like this:

1

    1.1

    1.2

2

    2.1

    2.2

        2.2.1

        2.2.2

Single digits indicate the project outline's highest task level; two digits indicate the second highest task level, and so on. Microsoft Project has built-in features for applying and customizing WBS code that let you create a code prefix, determine whether to use numbers or letters, establish the maximum number of characters that you can use at each level of code, and decide what character (such as a period or a slash) to use to separate the levels of code.

To apply WBS code structure to the tasks in your project, follow these steps:

1. Choose Project⇨WBS⇨Define Code from the menu bar. The WBS Code Definition dialog box appears.

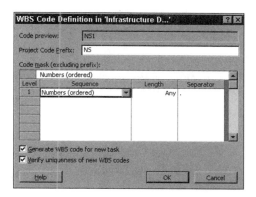

2. (Optional) Type a prefix in the Project Code Prefix text box. This prefix can be, for example, the project's name or an abbreviation that represents the project.

3. In the Code Mask field, click in the Level 1 row in the Sequence column. A drop-down list appears.

4. Select the sequence of characters you want to use for tasks at this level (numbers, upper or lowercase letters, or any character). If you choose this sequence, an asterisk appears at that level in the outline. You can replace this asterisk by displaying a WBS Code column in your view and editing an individual task's WBS Code. When you do, all tasks at that level in that family of tasks take on this designation.

5. Click the Length column and, in the drop-down list that appears, choose whether your code length is unlimited or limited to from one to ten characters.

6. Click the Separator column and, in the drop-down list that appears, indicate what character (such as a period, hyphen, or slash) you want to use to separate the characters at this code level. Each code level can use a different separator.

7. If you want Project to apply automatically a WBS code to tasks that you add, make sure a check mark appears in the Generate WBS Code for New Task check box.

8. Repeat Steps 3 through 7 to set the WBS code for other level tasks.

9. After you finish, click OK.

To view the WBS code, simply display a layout that includes a WBS Code column. To add the WBS column to the Gantt Chart view, follow these steps:

1. Click the Gantt Chart icon in the View bar along the left side of the Project screen. The Gantt Chart view appears.

2. Right-click any column heading.

3. Choose Insert Column from the shortcut menu that pops up. The Insert Column dialog box appears.

4. Select WBS from the Field Name drop-down list.

5. Click OK. The WBS code column appears to the left of the column you right-clicked in Step 2.

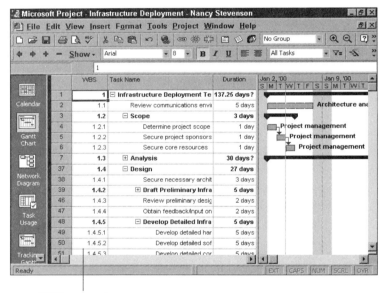

WBS code column

If you're going deeper than three or four task levels in your WBS code, you may want to consider breaking up your project into smaller projects. Too much detail and too many tasks can be cumbersome in a large project.

If you create several new tasks or delete some tasks after setting the WBS code, your WBS coding gets out of whack. New tasks have no code; other tasks have code, but it is no longer sequential. To redefine the code, select the specific tasks you want to renumber (to renumber the entire project, you don't need to select anything), and then follow these steps:

1. Choose Project➪WBS Code➪Renumber from the menu bar. The WBS Renumber dialog box appears.

2. Click to select either the Entire Project or the Selected Tasks radio button.

3. Click OK. Microsoft Project renumbers your WBS code.

Creating custom outline structures

In addition to the WBS outline structure that's built into Microsoft Project, you can create additional outline structures and customize them. For example, you may want to use a custom outline code that enables you to attach accounting codes to individual tasks so that you can sort the project to track costs by type.

Microsoft Project offers ten outline codes, which are identified as Outline Codes 1 through 10. You can rename these codes to clarify what the codes consist of, and you can determine their structure (whether the codes are numeric or alphabetic, for example) by following these steps:

1. Choose Tools➪Customize➪Fields from the menu bar. The Customize Fields dialog box appears.

2. In the Type drop-down list, select Outline Code to customize your outline code structure. A list of the ten outline codes appears.

3. Click to select one of the outline codes.

4. Click the Rename button. The Rename Field dialog box appears.

5. Type a name for the Code field.

6. Click OK.

7. Click the Define Outline Code button. The Code Definition dialog box appears.

8. Click in the Sequence column for Level 1. A drop-down list appears.

9. Select a Sequence structure for the first level of the code. You can choose numbers, uppercase or lowercase letters, or characters; characters enable you to replace a wildcard asterisk with any character you want.

10. From the drop-down lists in their respective columns, select a maximum Length of characters and a character (+, /, -, or .) to act as the Separator for this level of the code.

11. Repeat Steps 8 through 10 for each level of your outline.

12. Click OK to return to the Customize Fields dialog box.

13. Click OK to save the newly named and edited code.

You can view any code field by choosing Insert⇨Column from the menu bar and then selecting the column by name in the Insert Column dialog box.

Deleting Tasks

Deleting a task is as simple as selecting the task and then pressing the delete key. However, you need to be aware that deleting tasks can affect your outline.

If you delete a subtask, your outline code — including WBS code — may become out of sync. If that happens, you can easily fix the outline code by using the WBS Renumbering feature covered earlier in this part. If, however, you delete a summary task, the Planning Wizard brings up a dialog box to warn you that deleting a summary task also deletes its subtasks. You then have two choices: You can delete the summary task and all its subtasks, or you can cancel the operation.

Because the sole purpose of the Wizard's dialog box is to inform you that deleting a summary task also deletes its subtasks, you can indicate that you don't want to see this warning again. However, if someone else (who doesn't know Microsoft Project as well as you do) works on your schedule, that person won't see this warning either.

Displaying and Hiding Outline Levels

At certain times throughout your project, looking at all the subtasks (or at a particular phase of a project) can be helpful. At other times you may want to review only higher-level summary tasks because summary tasks provide a speedy snapshot of your project by summarizing the cost and timing of all the subtasks.

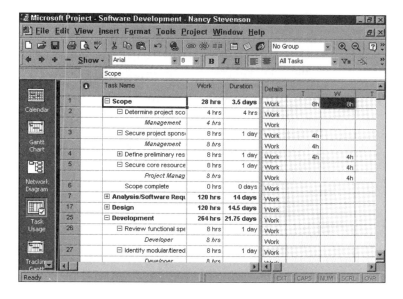

To display or hide various levels of a Project outline, you can choose from among the following options:

✔ To display the subtasks of a summary task with a task column in any view or in the Network view, click the view icon in the View bar. Then click the plus symbol that appears to the left of the summary task. As soon as the subtasks are displayed, the plus symbol becomes a minus symbol. To hide the summary task's subtasks, click the minus symbol.

✔ To display all the tasks in your project, click the Show button on the Formatting toolbar and then click All Subtasks.

✔ To display all project tasks up to a certain level, click the Show button and select a level from 1 to 10.

✔ To hide some of the levels, click the Show button and choose a lower outline level. To hide all levels, click the Hide Subtasks button.

Another method for displaying all your project's tasks quickly is to create an upper-level task summarizing all the other tasks in your project. Then you can click to select that task and in the Show drop-down list, select All Tasks to see every level of task in your entire project.

For more information about working with outlines, check out *Microsoft Project 2000 Bible,* by Elaine Marmel, published by IDG Books Worldwide, Inc.

Inserting Subprojects

Projects are often compiled piecemeal, with different managers building different phases of the project. Fortunately, inserting a subproject into another schedule to assemble all tasks into a final plan is simple. To insert a subproject, follow these steps:

1. Click the Gantt Chart icon in the View bar along the left side of the Project screen. The Gantt Chart view appears.

2. Click the task that is one level above where you want to insert the subproject. For example, if the project you're inserting is one of the ten main project phases, click the highest-level task. If the project you're inserting is part of the second phase of your schedule, click the second-phase summary task.

3. Choose Insert⇨Project. The Insert Project dialog box appears.

4. Click the Project file you want to insert.

5. Click the Insert button to insert the file. The project is inserted into your schedule.

Note: You can also click the arrow next to the Insert button and choose Insert Read-Only from a drop-down list. This means that no changes can be made to that project information from this file.

If you think you may need to insert one project into another, you can create an upper-level task under which all your other tasks fall. That way, the subproject you insert is clearly organized as a separate phase of your project.

Moving Tasks

As you work on a project, you often need to rearrange tasks. To rearrange tasks in Project, you can

- Demote some tasks (indenting) to move the tasks down one level in the outline hierarchy

- Promote some tasks (outdenting) to move the tasks around the different levels of your outline hierarchy

- Eliminate some tasks altogether (which works differently for subtasks than for summary tasks)

Demoting tasks

Demoting a task indents that task one level in the outline hierarchy and turns the task into a subtask to the task above it. Keep in mind that a task can be both a subtask of a summary task and a summary task of a lower-level subtask at the same time. To demote a task, follow these steps:

1. Make sure the task you want to demote appears beneath the task that you want as its summary task.

2. Select the task you want to demote.

 3. Click the Indent button on the Formatting toolbar. Microsoft Project demotes your task.

 When you first insert a new task, it appears in your outline structure at the same level as the task you select when you perform the insert. So, if you want to create a level 3 task, select an existing level 3 task before you insert the new task. That way, the new task appears at the correct level, which can save you the trouble of demoting or promoting the task later.

Promoting tasks

Sometimes you may demote a task in your outline only to find that you want to move that task to a higher level. To promote a task, simply follow these steps:

1. Select the task you want to promote.

 2. Click the Outdent button on the Formatting toolbar. Microsoft Project promotes your task.

Cutting and pasting tasks

When rearranging tasks in your project, you can move a task simply by cutting and pasting it into a new location. Just follow these steps:

1. Highlight the task you want to move.

 2. Click the Cut button on the toolbar. The task is removed from its original location.

3. Place your cursor on the task above the spot where you want to position the task you're moving.

 4. Click the Paste button on the toolbar. The task you're moving appears above the task where you previously placed your cursor and at that task's same level in the outline.

 You can reverse many actions simply by clicking the Undo button.

Moving subtasks

Perhaps the easiest method of moving summary tasks around your outline, if you're not moving them very far, is to drag and drop them. You can also easily move subtasks from one location to another under a summary task or from one summary task to another. When you move a subtask, that subtask appears at the same level as the tasks where you moved it. To move a subtask, just follow these steps:

1. Click the gray selection area on the far-left side of the task row to select the row you want to move.

2. Hold down your left mouse button and drag the task from its original location. A long, gray, horizontal line, which represents the task, appears.

3. After you position the gray line where you want the task to appear, release your mouse button.

Moving summary tasks

Moving summary tasks is different from moving subtasks. When you move a summary task, its subtasks move with it. If you want to move a summary task without moving its subtasks, you have two choices: You can go to the trouble of promoting every subtask beneath the summary task, which frees the summary task from the subtasks so you can move it. An easier method, however, is to create a new summary task for the existing subtasks, which enables you to move the original summary task without moving the subtasks. You can move the task by using either the cut-and-paste or drag-and-drop method. *See also* "Demoting tasks" and "Promoting tasks" earlier in this part.

Part IV

Setting Timing with Dependencies, Constraints, and Deadlines

A ssigning a specific duration for each of your project tasks is only the tip of the timing iceberg in Microsoft Project 2000. If, when you set duration, every task in your project starts on the same day, your entire project will take as long as its longest task. To truly see the overall timing of a series of tasks, you have to do more than assign task durations. You have to work with timing relationships between tasks and with the constraints and deadlines that are associated with each task. These relationships control when tasks can and can't occur concurrently, thereby creating a schedule that reflects the overall timing of your project. In this part you discover how to set the dependencies, constraints, and deadlines that control your project timing.

In this part . . .

Creating Dependencies between Projects

You usually don't plan projects in a vacuum. Instead, you share resources (and sometimes deadlines) with others in your organization who are working on other projects or with several projects under your control. With Microsoft Project, you can coordinate the timing of your project's tasks with the timing of other projects. When you link projects this way, any schedule change in an external project is reflected automatically in your schedule's timing. To make such updates, the external schedule must be available to your project file. You can make project files available to more than one project manager by using a company intranet, posting files on an Internet site, or regularly exchanging updated schedules with other project managers by using e-mail and updating your project file on your hard drive.

Linking tasks in different projects

One method of establishing dependencies between or among projects is to establish links between tasks in your project and tasks in other projects. To establish a task link, follow these steps:

1. Open both project files and display the Gantt Chart view by clicking the Gantt Chart icon in the View bar along the left side of the Project screen.

2. Choose Window➪Arrange All from the menu bar so that both projects are visible.

3. Double-click in the Task Name column for the task you want to link as a successor to a task in another project. The Task Information dialog box appears.

4. Click the Predecessors tab.

5. In the ID and Task Name columns, type the ID number and the path and project name of the task you want to link to (for example, type **110** and **c:/projects/DesignPrototype**).

6. In the Type and Lag fields, adjust the dependency to create the relationship you want. Doing this involves defining one of four types of timing relationships and entering the lag time, if any, between the two tasks. *See also* "Creating Dependencies between Tasks" later in this part.

7. Click OK.

   After you create a link, Microsoft Project informs you of any change in the timing of the linked external task that impacts your schedule. When you open your schedule with the other project available, a dialog box appears informing you of the change in the external schedule and giving you the option of allowing the change or not.

Representing an external dependency with a milestone

Another way to establish a timing relationship between projects is to create a new milestone in your schedule. A milestone is a task of no duration and represents the moment in time when an external project is complete. For example, if your project is to install a network in a new building, you can include a milestone (called Building Construction, for example) that reflects an external project dealing with the building's construction. If you link the start of your network installation to this task, the automatic updating that a link causes keeps you from beginning installation before the building construction is complete. Some people prefer using the milestone method — which flags changes in another project's completion — rather than linking to individual tasks in other projects. *See also* information on milestones in Part II.

One way to use a milestone is to create and link a milestone in your project to another project's highest-level summary task. That way, any shift on the part of the milestone indicates that the completion of the other project has in fact been delayed. Another method is to link to the last task in the project, again reflecting the completion of the external project in your own.

To create a milestone, follow these steps:

1. Choose Insert➪New Task from the menu bar. A blank row for the new task appears in the spreadsheet.

2. Type a name for the task in the Task Name column.

3. Type **0** in the Duration column.

4. Click OK to save the task and then follow the steps in "Linking Tasks between Projects" in this part.

Creating Dependencies between Tasks

A dependency relationship is a timing relationship. Establishing a dependency link between two tasks sets a rule that governs when one task finishes or starts in relation to another task. The first task is the predecessor, and the second is the successor. After you set a dependency between two tasks, the position of the two taskbars graphically depicts the relationship.

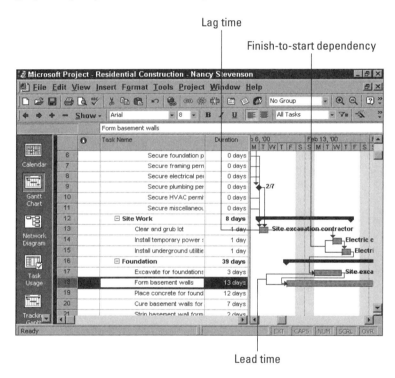

Lag time

Finish-to-start dependency

Lead time

Microsoft Project offers you a choice of the following four standard dependencies:

✔ **Finish-to-Start.** In this common dependency (which is the default and therefore easiest to set in Microsoft Project), the first task must finish before the next task can start. An example of a finish-to-start relationship is getting a building permit (the predecessor) before starting construction of an office building (the successor).

🖝 **Finish-to-Finish.** In this dependency, one task can't finish until another task does. Project forces the successor task to end at the same time as the predecessor task. For example, if you want both a brochure and a product package shipped to a printer to be printed together for cost savings, you can set a finish-to-finish relationship in the brochure and packaging task dates.

🖝 **Start-to-Finish.** In this dependency, the successor task can finish only after the predecessor starts. A delay in the predecessor's start causes a delay in the successor's finish. For example, if you want to conduct employee training as close as possible to the installation date for new software so that the information is still fresh, a start-to-finish relationship between training and implementation can be just the thing.

🖝 **Start-to-Start.** In this dependency, two tasks start at the same time, such as an ad campaign in which TV and print ads start simultaneously to make the greatest marketing impact.

You can also set lead time (in which the relationship is set by deducting time from another task's start or finish, often causing an overlap between two tasks) or lag time (in which the relationship is established by adding time to the start or finish of another task causing a delay between the end of one task and the start of another). *See also* "Setting lead or lag time" later in this part.

Setting a dependency relationship

To set a dependency relationship, follow these steps:

1. Click the Gantt Chart icon in the View bar along the left side of the Project screen. The Gantt Chart view appears.

2. Double-click the task you want to set as the Successor. The Task Information dialog box appears.

3. Click the Predecessors tab.

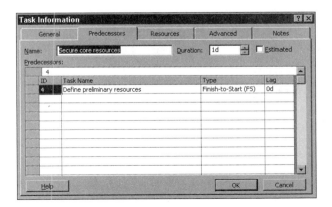

4. Click the first blank Task Name cell. A drop-down list appears.

5. Select the task with which you want to set the relationship or enter the task's ID number, if you know it.

6. Click the Type column and from the drop-down list that appears, select the dependency relationship you want: Finish-to-Start (FS), Finish-to-Finish (FF), Start-to-Finish (SF), or Start-to-Start (SS).

7. Click OK to set the relationship.

When you return to the Gantt Chart view, you see the dependency relationship graphically represented in the position of the two taskbars.

 Microsoft offers a Link tool that automatically sets the Finish-to-Start dependency, which is one of the most common dependency relationships. This tool can't be used to set any other dependency type.

To set a Finish-to-Start dependency by using the Link tool, follow these steps:

1. Click the Gantt Chart icon in the View bar along the left side of the Project screen. The Gantt Chart view appears.

2. Select two or more tasks in a project. If you want to select non-adjacent tasks, hold down the Ctrl key as you click your selections.

 3. Click the Link Tasks button on the Formatting toolbar.

 Microsoft Project 2000 has a new feature called Fill. Fill copies information from one task to another. If you set a dependency relationship for two tasks and want to apply that same relationship to several subsequent tasks, display either the successor or predecessor column. Click in the column for the task you want to copy and drag the fill handle that appears at the bottom right corner of the cell to highlight as many tasks beneath it as you want. The same dependency relationship is created throughout that series of tasks.

 For more information about all the dependency types, see *Microsoft Project 2000 Bible,* by Elaine Marmel, published by IDG Books Worldwide, Inc.

Setting lead or lag time

In addition to setting the four standard dependencies, you can also designate lead time (in which you subtract time from the start or finish of one task to establish the timing of another) or lag time (in which you add time to the start or finish of one task to establish the timing of another). If you establish a finish-to-start relationship, for example, and you add a week's delay (lag), the successor task starts one week after the predecessor finishes. If you set a finish-to-start relationship and then insert four days of lead time, the successor task starts four days before the end of the predecessor task, thereby creating an overlap between the two tasks.

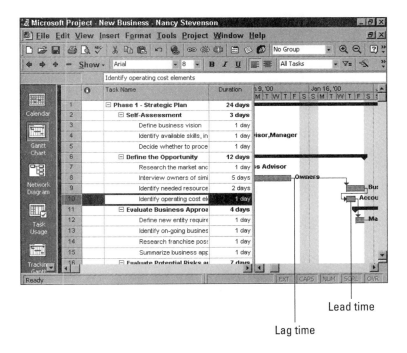

Lead time

Lag time

To add lead or lag time to a dependency relationship, follow these steps:

1. Click the Gantt Chart icon in the View bar along the left side of the Project screen. The Gantt Chart view appears.

2. Double-click the successor task. The Task Information dialog box appears.

3. Click the Predecessors tab.

4. In the Lag column, click the task dependency you want to change. *Note:* Although the column is titled Lag, both lag and lead time are controlled by settings in this column.

5. By using the spinner arrows in the Lag column, set a positive number for lag time or a negative number for lead time.

6. Click OK.

After you add a lead or lag time, you may get a dialog box indicating that a task now starts before the project start date. You can then choose to let the task begin earlier than the project's official start date, to change your project start date accordingly, or to cancel or modify the dependency relationship.

Deleting a Dependency

To delete a dependency between tasks, complete the following steps:

1. Click the Gantt Chart icon in the View bar along the left side of the Project screen. The Gantt Chart view appears.

2. Double-click the task for which you want to delete a dependency. The Task Information dialog box appears.

3. Click the Predecessors tab.

4. In the Type column, click the row for the dependency you want to delete.

5. In the drop-down list that appears, click None.

6. Click OK.

Another way to delete dependencies between tasks is to select a task in the Gantt Chart view and click the Unlink tool on the Formatting toolbar. Doing so, however, deletes all task dependencies for that task. To delete a single dependency between two tasks, select both tasks and then use the Unlink tool.

Establishing Constraints

Like dependency relationships, constraints affect task timing. However, a constraint sets a timing relationship to a calendar date rather than to another task. By its nature, a constraint is less fluid than a dependency.

If you create a new task and schedule it based on the project's start date, the As Soon As Possible constraint applies by default. This means the task occurs as soon as it can, according to other parameters that you apply. If you create a new task and schedule it based on the project's finish date, the As Late As Possible constraint applies by default. You can apply to a task the following types of constraints:

🖛 **As Late As Possible:** Schedules the task to occur as late in your schedule as possible, based on any other timing parameters.

✔ **As Soon as Possible:** Schedules the task to occur as early in your schedule as possible, based on any other timing parameters.

✔ **Finish No Earlier Than:** Determines the earliest date on which a task can end.

✔ **Finish No Later Than:** Sets the latest date by which a task must be completed. However, the task can be completed anytime before that date.

✔ **Must Finish On:** Specifies an absolute constraint on the date on which a task must end. This constraint cannot be overridden by other parameters.

✔ **Must Start On:** Specifies an absolute constraint on the date on which a task must begin. This constraint takes precedence over any other timing parameter you apply.

✔ **Start No Earlier Than:** Determines the earliest date on which a task can start.

✔ **Start No Later Than:** Sets the latest date by which a task must start.

Although dependencies, constraints, and start and finish dates work in concert to determine your tasks' timing, constraints are the least flexible feature for finding the fastest way to complete your project or avoid resource overallocations. In addition, a constraint doesn't necessarily adjust a task's timing if tasks preceding the constrained task are completed early or put on hold. Sometimes, however, you may find the inflexibility desirable. For example, if you're planning the Macy's Thanksgiving Day Parade, you don't want the parade to take place any later than Thanksgiving, even if one float isn't ready. So apply constraints carefully, making them the exception rather than the rule.

To set a constraint, follow these steps:

1. Click the Gantt Chart icon in the View bar along the left side of the Project screen. The Gantt Chart view appears.

2. Double-click the task for which you want to set the constraint. The Task Information dialog box appears.

3. Click the Advanced tab.

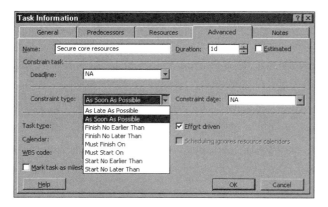

4. Click the arrow in the Constraint Type field and select an option from the drop-down list.

5. Click the arrow in the Constraint Date field and then click the date for your constraint in the drop-down calendar.

6. Click OK.

Setting Deadlines

Unlike the Must Finish On constraint that absolutely controls the finish date of a task, setting a deadline doesn't control the task's timing. A deadline merely causes an indicator to appear if a task isn't completed by a scheduled date.

Using a project deadline instead of a constraint allows Microsoft Project to manipulate a date to help deal with resource overloads or changes in other timing parameters.

To set a deadline, follow these steps:

1. Click the Gantt Chart icon in the View bar along the left side of the Project screen. The Gantt Chart view appears.

2. Double-click the task for which you want to set a deadline. The Task Information dialog box appears.

3. Click the Advanced tab.

4. Click the arrow in the Deadline field and select a deadline date from the drop-down calendar.

5. Click OK.

Part V

Defining Resources

Few project managers can complete a project without help.
Resources are the people, equipment, materials, and even the
facilities that you use to help you accomplish your project goals.
When you create a resource in Microsoft Project, you need to provide information about the nature, availability, and costs
associated with that resource. This part deals with creating your
own resources and sharing resources that exist in other projects,
as well as working with several Project features to set resource
availability and specify resource working hours.

In this part . . .

Adding Resource Notes

To the individual resources you create in Microsoft Project, you can attach notes about abilities, interests, equipment models, managers to contact, and so on. To do so, follow these steps:

1. Click the Resource Sheet icon in the View bar along the left side of the Project screen. The Resource Sheet view appears.

2. Right-click a resource in the Resource Name column and select Resource Notes from the shortcut menu. The Resource dialog box appears with the Notes tab displayed.

3. Enter your notes.

4. Use the formatting tools across the top of the Notes text box to format selected text for readability or aesthetics. You can adjust font, text alignment, and bulleted-list formatting.

5. Click OK.

After you add a resource note, you can view the note by right-clicking a resource in the Resource Name column and using the shortcut menu that appears or by clicking the Resource Information button and then clicking the Notes tab.

Borrowing Resources from Other Projects

If several projects need to share resources, you can save time by creating a Project file that contains one set of resources, called a resource pool, for your company's project managers to use. You can then use the resource-sharing capabilities of Microsoft Project to make the resources you saved in that file available to other Project files. This saves you and others from having to create these resources over and over again in separate projects.

In addition, creating resources in a central file and sharing them among projects can also lend consistency across projects because settings such as costs, availability, and nonworking time can be kept the same across your company.

Creating a resource pool

You create a resource pool by opening a new Project file, entering the resource information, and saving the file. You can then easily make this resource-pool file available on your network or over the Internet to every project manager in your company, rather than simply sharing the file with other projects on a case-by-case basis. *See also* Part XIII for more on sharing information.

To create a resource-pool file, follow these steps:

1. Click the New button on the Standard toolbar. The Project Information dialog box appears.

2. Click OK to close the dialog box without changing any settings. You now have a new, blank Project file on-screen.

3. Save the file with any name that identifies it as a file containing resource information.

4. Click Save.

5. Click the Resource Sheet icon in the View bar along the left side of the Project screen. The Resource Sheet view appears.

6. Choose View⇨Table⇨Entry from the menu bar. A new table of the Resource Sheet view appears with columns that make entering resource information easy.

7. Enter all resource-pool information. If you need to add resource details, you can either use additional columns or double-click each resource name and enter information in the Resource Information dialog box that appears.

8. Click Save to save the file.

Using a shared resource pool

When you choose to share a pool of resources, you need to decide how to resolve conflicts that may occur between resource calendars or other resource information in your project file versus that same information in the resource-pool file. You can establish that the settings in the resource pool take precedence, or you can let settings in your project override the settings in the resource-pool file.

To share resources contained in a resource pool with your own project, follow these steps:

1. Choose File⇨Open from the menu bar. The Open dialog box appears.

2. Click the project filename to open it.

3. Again, choose File⇨Open from the menu bar.

4. In the Open dialog box that appears, click the resource-pool filename to open it.

5. With your project file open, choose Tools⇨Resources⇨Share Resources. The Share Resources dialog box appears.

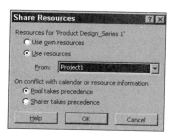

6. Click to select the Use Resources radio button.

7. In the From drop-down list, select the resource-pool file.

8. Click to select either the Pool Takes Precedence or Sharer Takes Precedence radio button to establish how you want Project to deal with conflicts.

9. Click OK.

Creating Individual Resources

Resources can be people, equipment, materials, facilities, and anything else that you need to help you complete the tasks in your project. Microsoft Project enables you to create as many resources as you want for a project. When you create resources, you need to specify whether they are work resources or material resources. If they are work resources, you need to specify their names and how to contact them.

Entering resource name and contact information

To create a resource, you open a new Resource Information dialog box and type the general information about the resource, such as the person's name and e-mail address. To do this, follow these steps:

1. Click the Resource Sheet icon in the View bar along the left side of the Project screen. The Resource Sheet view appears.

2. Double-click an empty cell in the Resource Name column. The Resource Information dialog box appears.

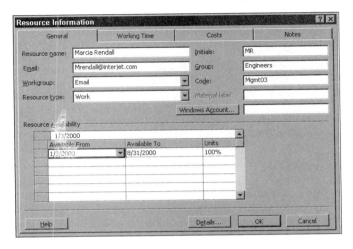

3. Click the General tab.

4. Type a resource name in the Resource Name text box.

5. Type an e-mail address in the Email text box.

6. Type initials or another abbreviation in the Initials text box and a code in the Code text box, if you want.

7. If you're using Project Central to communicate with your project resources, you can type an identification in the Windows Account text box that allows you to log on to the Central server. *See also* Part XIII for information on Project Central.

8. Click OK to save the resource.

You can also enter new resource information by displaying the Resource Sheet view and typing information directly into the columns that appear. This method is faster, but not all information available by default in the Resource Information form is included in this view. If you're new to creating resources, initially use the preceding method. After you're familiar with the typical resource information fields, then you can work with additional columns in the Resource Sheet view.

Although entering resource initials is helpful because you can work with narrower columns and fit more columns into a report or on-screen, be careful. In a large project, a lot of people may have the same initials, so you may get confused about which resource is assigned to which task. Using an abbreviation or a nickname is sometimes more helpful.

Creating consolidated resources

Consolidated resources, also called resource groups, are typically sets of individuals or items that are often assigned to perform some task together, such as a cleanup crew, a fleet of company vehicles, or a clerical pool. (Don't confuse consolidated resources with the Project feature for grouping resources, which is simply a way of adding a group affiliation to a resource and then sorting tasks by those affiliations.) By creating one resource to represent a group, you save time when making assignments to multiple project tasks because you don't have to retype individual names for each resource.

To create a consolidated resource, follow the steps in the "Entering resource name and contact information" section earlier in this part and then assign a filename that represents a group rather than an individual. Be sure to take into account the number of resources in your consolidated resource when you specify the maximum units of time that a resource is available to your project — for example, a group with eight full-time resources has available units of 800 percent. *See also* "Setting resource availability" later in this part for information on specifying resource maximum units.

Choosing the resource type

A new feature in Microsoft Project 2000 enables you to divide your resources into two groups: work resources and material resources. Because work resources are typically people, their files should include contact information and the dates and amount of time they're available to work. When you designate a work resource, you can modify that resource's calendar on the Working Time tab in the Resource Information dialog box.

A material resource represents materials, such as steel beams, that you use on your tasks. If you establish a material resource, the General tab in the Resource Information dialog box doesn't include contact fields, such as Email and Windows Account. The General tab does, however, contain a Material Label text box in which you can enter units (such as pounds or square feet) or a phonetic code and then search by phonetic strings (for example, for material resources with foreign syllables in their names). Also, the Working Time tab in the Resource Information dialog box obviously isn't an option when you create a material resource — because materials don't get days off!

To create a resource type, follow these steps:

1. Click the Resource Sheet icon in the View bar along the left side of the Project screen. The Resource Sheet view appears.

2. Double-click an existing resource. The Resource Information dialog box appears.

3. Click the General tab.

4. In the Resource Type field, select Material or Work.

5. Click OK.

 Tip: You can also display the Resource Information dialog box by selecting a resource in the Resource Sheet view and clicking the Resource Information button on the Standard toolbar. The Resource Information dialog box appears, showing the tab you last displayed.

Grouping Resources

Many resources fall into logical groupings, such as engineers, contract employees, or factory workers. By entering a group name or code when you create a resource, you can sort, apply a filter so only tasks that meet specified criteria are shown, and group resources by that name or code. You can also perform the same operations on tasks, based on the group resources assigned to them. For example, if a set of workers in your operation gets a pay-rate increase, you can search for all the tasks they're working on to make necessary adjustments to the task files.

To assign a resource to a group, follow these steps:

1. Click the Resource Sheet icon in the View bar along the left side of the Project screen. The Resource Sheet view appears.

2. Double-click the name of the resource you want to assign to a group. The Resource Information dialog box appears.

3. Click the General tab and type a group name in the Group text box.

4. Click OK.

After assigning a group resource, you can use the standard sort and filter features with the group criterion. Sorting organizes tasks by a criterion, such as alphabetically by group affiliation, and filtering removes any tasks that don't match the group criterion from your screen. You can also organize the resources on a Resource Sheet by grouping them. To do so, choose Project⇨Group by⇨Resource Group. *See also* Part VIII for more information on filtering.

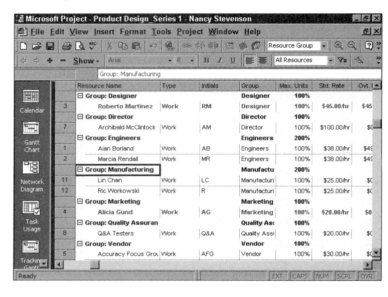

Resource Calendars

When you assign a resource to a task, Microsoft Project enables you to modify that resource's calendar a number of ways. You can set a resource's availability to work on the project, specify the resource's working hours, or block off specific periods of time during which the resource may be unavailable (such as holidays and vacation time). Project takes into account the resource's calendar settings when it calculates a task's cost and timing.

Setting resource availability

Microsoft Project enables you to specify date ranges for a resource's availability for your project, including time variables. For example, a resource who is a professor on an academic project may be on sabbatical half the year and only available to work part-time. In such a case, you need to indicate multiple settings for resource availability.

Resource calendars are vital to your project's cost and timing accuracy. When you enter resource time spent on a task, Project calculates a day of resource effort based on the resource's calendar. A $20-an-hour resource who is working one four-hour day does not cost the same as a $20-an-hour resource who is working on an eight-hour-day calendar. In tracking whether an effort-driven task is complete, Project recognizes only four hours of completed effort when you indicate that your half-time resource has worked one day; therefore, the task will take longer to complete using that resource.

To set a resource's project availability, follow these steps:

1. Click the Resource Sheet icon in the View bar along the left side of the Project screen. The Resource Sheet view appears.

2. Double-click the resource you want to edit. The Resource Information dialog box appears.

3. Click the General tab.

4. In the Resource Availability field, click to select the first blank cell in the Available From column and type a start date.

5. In the same row, in the Available To column, click to select the blank cell and type the end date for the resource's availability.

6. In the same row, in the Units column, click to select the blank cells and type the resource's percentage of available time.

7. Click OK.

Changing the resource base calendar

To set resource working time and avoid overallocation, you can customize a base calendar for each resource. To set a resource base calendar, follow these steps:

1. Click the Resource Sheet icon in the View bar along the left side of the Project screen. The Resource Sheet view appears.

2. Double-click a resource name in the Resource Name column. The Resource Information dialog box appears.

3. Click the Working Time tab.

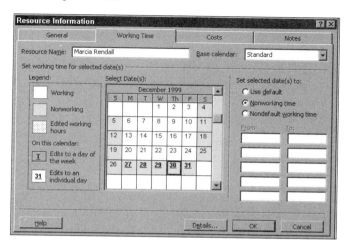

4. Click the drop-down list in the Base Calendar field.

5. Click the calendar you prefer for this resource. Project offers you the following options:

   • **Standard:** 8:00 a.m. to 5:00 p.m., with an hour break

   • **24 Hours:** 24-hour workday, with no breaks

   • **Night Shift:** Midnight to 8:00 a.m., with an hour break

6. Click OK.

After you set a base calendar, you can make changes to customize the resource's calendar, such as setting a certain day of the week as a nonworking day or a particular hour of the day as a nonworking hour.

Specifying working and nonworking hours

Although a base calendar lets you set a resource's typical work hours, every resource has variables, such as company holidays, personal vacations, a weekday that the resource works part-time, leaves of absence, and so on. When these situations occur, you have to modify working and nonworking hours for that specific period for an individual resource, overriding the base calendar for that time. You do this by following these steps:

1. Click the Resource Sheet icon in the View bar along the left side of the Project screen. The Resource Sheet view appears.

2. Double-click a resource to open the Resource Information dialog box.

3. Click the Working Time tab.

4. By using the scroll bar, locate a month you want to modify.

5. Select a date (or dates).

6. In the Set Selected Date(s) To area, click to change the selection of one of the following radio buttons (if necessary):

   • **Use Default:** Specifies no change in the default hours (based on the resource calendar)

   • **Nonworking Time:** Specifies nonworking days

   • **Nondefault Working Time:** Specifies days on which the resource works different hours from the default hours (based on the resource base calendar)

   If you choose Nondefault Working Time, click the From text box to type a start time and then click the To text box to type an end time for the resource's workday. If the workday includes lengthy breaks, you can set two or more segments of work time by using successive From and To text boxes.

7. Click OK.

Try not to micromanage resource calendars. If a resource attends a seminar for a day but can finish your task on time, don't bother marking that one day as nonworking time. You need to change a resource calendar only if someone works an odd schedule on a regular basis or takes a two- or three-week absence from work.

Part VI

Associating Resources with Costs

One of the most useful features in Microsoft Project is the capability to tally your project costs — which Microsoft Project does by associating costs with resources — to help you keep track of your budget. In this part you find out how to assign costs to resources and how to identify the fixed costs incurred during your project.

In this part . . .

Creating Fixed Costs

Most projects incur fixed costs, which are set amounts (such as fees for construction permits or airfare) as opposed to variable time or usage costs. A fixed cost is attached to an individual task and included in task- and project-cost calculations. In Microsoft Project, you can assign only one fixed cost per task. However, if you have several fixed costs, you can simply make one of them the total of several fixed costs and then keep a tally of individual costs in your task notes.

TIP

You can also deal with recurring fixed costs by creating a resource that you assign to your tasks. That way, for example, if you make frequent trips to a site and airfare runs $400, you can create a resource called Site Visits, assign a $400 per use resource cost, and then assign that resource to any task you want.

To create a fixed cost, follow these steps:

1. Click the Gantt Chart icon in the View bar along the left side of the Project screen. The Gantt Chart view appears.

2. Choose View➪Table➪Cost. The Cost Table appears in the spreadsheet portion of the Gantt Chart view.

3. Click in the Fixed Cost column in the task you want to assign the cost to.

4. Type the fixed-cost amount.

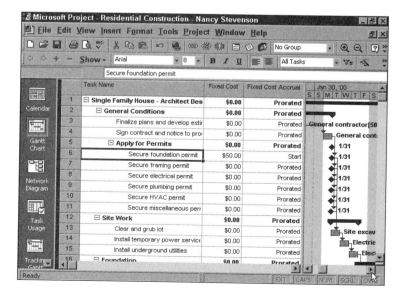

You may also consider adding some fixed costs to your project's summary task. For instance, if you want to budget $10,000 for phone calls, you add that fixed cost to your highest-level task rather than assigning several separate costs to specific tasks.

Entering Per Use Costs

You can create a resource and assign that resource a per use cost, which will be incurred each time you use the resource (such as a repair person's visit or a meeting-facility rental). To create a resource with a per use cost, follow these steps:

1. Click the Resource Sheet icon in the View bar along the left side of the Project screen. The Resource Sheet view appears.

2. Double-click a blank Resource Name cell or an existing resource. The Resource Information dialog box appears.

3. Click the Costs tab.

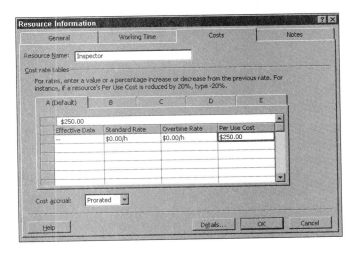

4. Click the Per Use Cost column and type in an amount.

5. In the Cost Accrual drop-down list, select the cost-accrual method.

6. Click OK.

Establishing Standard and Overtime Rates

People who are assigned as resources, and occasionally other kinds of resources, are charged at an hourly rate and have a higher rate if they work overtime. After you record a resource's activity on a task, Project multiplies the number of hours worked by each resource's hourly rate to calculate a cost.

Microsoft Project doesn't automatically apply overtime rates after you enter a resource activity for a task, so you have to manually calculate overtime. *See also* Part XI for more about how to do this.

Entering default resource rates

To enter standard and overtime rates for a resource, follow these steps:

1. Click the Resource Sheet icon in the View bar along the left side of the Project screen. The Resource Sheet view appears.

2. Double-click a Resource Name cell to open the Resource Information dialog box for that resource.

3. Click the Costs tab.

4. Click in the first row in the Standard Rate column on Tab A (Default) and type a rate and a timeframe (such as $25.00/h for twenty-five dollars an hour). You can enter rates in minutes, hours, days, and years (m/h/d/y).

5. Click in the Overtime Rate column and type an overtime rate and a timeframe.

6. If you want to set a different default rate for a specific future date, click in the second row in the Effective Date column and set a date in the drop-down calendar that appears.

7. Type standard and overtime rates in the appropriate columns of the second row of the rate table. Repeat this procedure in successive rows to set as many rate/time periods (up to 25) as you want.

8. Click OK.

When entering a material resource rate, you need to enter a number only, because time isn't a factor. For example, if you pay $250 per box of tool bits, your standard rate is $250. However, if you assign the material cost to a task at 200 percent, then the cost comes to $500 for two boxes.

Entering nondefault resource rates

Sometimes resources are charged at different rates, depending on what task they're working on. For example, an employee working on an in-house marketing project may be charged at a lower rate than that same employee working on a marketing job for a client. In such cases, you may need to enter more than one set of rates for a resource.

To enter nondefault rates in the cost rate table, follow these steps:

1. Click the Resource Sheet icon in the View bar along the left side of the Project screen. The Resource Sheet view appears.

2. In the Resource Name column, double-click the name of the resource you want to edit. The Resource Information dialog box appears.

3. Click the Costs tab.

4. Click Tab B, C, D, or E.

5. Type the standard and overtime rates in the appropriate columns.

6. Click OK.

You can display cost rate tables in the Resource Sheet view. To do so, click in the column to the left of where you want the new column to appear, choose Insert⇨Column, and click the Cost Rate Table column.

Setting the Cost-Accrual Method

Each resource has an associated accrual method. This method determines when the costs that are assigned to a task will accrue. By default, a cost is prorated throughout the life of the task, which simply means that at any stage of a task's progress, accrued costs are prorated along with the amount of work done to date.

If the default accrual method isn't what you want, you can set the accrual method either to Start (all the costs accrue as soon as the task begins) or End (all the costs accrue after the task is completed). For example, if you have a cost that isn't billed until the work is done, you probably want to select the End option.

 If you assign a per use cost to a resource, the cost always accrues when the task starts.

To change the fixed-cost accrual method, follow these steps:

1. Click the Gantt Chart icon in the View bar along the left side of the Project screen. The Gantt Chart view appears.

2. Choose View⬦Table⬦Cost. The Cost Table appears in the spreadsheet of the Gantt Chart view.

3. Click in the Fixed Cost Accrual column in the row for the task you want to change. A drop-down list appears.

4. Select the accrual method you prefer.

To change the accrual method for hourly resources or resources that are assigned a Per Use cost, follow these steps:

1. Click the Resource Sheet icon in the View bar along the left side of the Project screen. The Resource Sheet view appears.

2. In the Resource Name column, double-click the resource you want to edit. The Resource Information dialog box appears.

3. Click the Costs tab.

4. In the Cost Accrual drop-down list, select an accrual method.

5. Click OK.

Viewing Resource Cost Information

After you assign cost rates to resources, you may want to review the rates. Here's a quick and easy way to do so:

1. Click the Resource Sheet icon in the View bar along the left side of the Project screen. The Resource Sheet view appears.

2. Choose View⬦Table⬦Entry. The Entry Table appears in the spreadsheet section of the Gantt Chart view.

   The Entry table shows all the rate information for resources (but doesn't include fixed costs, which are task-associated). *See also* "Creating Fixed Costs" earlier in this part for more information on how fixed costs work.

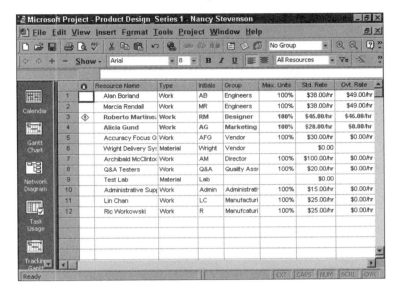

		❶	Resource Name	Type	Initials	Group	Max. Units	Std. Rate	Ovt. Rate
	1		Alan Borland	Work	AB	Engineers	100%	$38.00/hr	$49.00/hr
	2		Marcia Rendall	Work	MR	Engineers	100%	$38.00/hr	$49.00/hr
	3	◈	Roberto Martine:	Work	RM	Designer	100%	$46.00/hr	$46.00/hr
	4		Alicia Gund	Work	AG	Marketing	100%	$28.00/hr	$0.00/hr
	5		Accuracy Focus G	Work	AFG	Vendor	100%	$30.00/hr	$0.00/hr
	6		Wright Delivery Sy:	Material	Wright	Vendor		$0.00	
	7		Archibald McClinto:	Work	AM	Director	100%	$100.00/hr	$0.00/hr
	8		Q&A Testers	Work	Q&A	Quality Assi	100%	$20.00/hr	$0.00/hr
	9		Test Lab	Material	Lab			$0.00	
	10		Administrative Sup|	Work	Admin	Administrati	100%	$15.00/hr	$0.00/hr
	11		Lin Chan	Work	LC	Manufacturi	100%	$25.00/hr	$0.00/hr
	12		Ric Workowski	Work	R	Manufcaturi	100%	$25.00/hr	$0.00/hr

Part VII

Making Resource Assignments

A fter you create your project resources and associate those resources with costs, you need to assign your resources to their respective tasks. Assigning a resource is easy to do: Simply select a name from a list of resources and indicate the amount of time you expect that resource to work on a task. Microsoft Project helps you automate the process of informing people of their assignments, which they can either accept or decline. In this part you discover how to make resource assignments and how to communicate those assignments to your team.

In this part . . .

Accepting or Declining Assignments by E-Mail

When you send TeamAssign messages via e-mail to tell resources about task assignments, they can accept or decline their assignments by return e-mail. To do so, a resource on your project must follow these steps:

1. Double-click the TeamAssign message to open it.

2. (Optional) Type a response message in the message text box.

3. Accept the assignment by leaving the default Yes response in the Accept column or decline the assignment by typing **No** in the Accept column.

4. Click Reply. The TeamAssign response is mailed to the project manager's WebInBox.

If your team uses Microsoft Outlook as its e-mail provider and a resource accepts a task assignment, Outlook automatically adds the assignment to that person's Outlook task list.

See also Part XIII for more information about communicating with workgroups.

Assigning Resources

Some people prefer to pick one resource and assign that particular resource to all of his or her tasks throughout the project at one time. Others prefer to determine all the resources involved in a specific task, assign them all to that task at the same time, and then proceed through the project task by task until all assignments have been made. Whichever method you prefer, assigning resources for a large project can be a lengthy and somewhat tedious process. Keep in mind, however, that making these assignments helps you manage project costs so that the time you spend is worthwhile.

Assigning resources

To assign a resource that is already created to a task, follow these steps:

1. Click the Gantt Chart icon in the View bar along the left side of the Project screen. The Gantt Chart view appears.

2. Click the task to which you want to assign a resource.

3. Click the Assign Resources button on the Standard Toolbar. The Assign Resources dialog box appears.

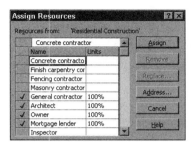

4. In the Name column, click the resource you want to assign to a task. If necessary, use the scroll bar on the right to locate the name.

5. Click Assign. A check mark indicating an assignment appears next to the resource name.

6. Click Close.

You can also use the Gantt Chart view to assign resources. To do so, choose View⟹Table⟹Entry and then type additional resource names in the Resource Name column for a specific task, separating resource names with a comma. This method is certainly faster, but be aware that all resources you enter this way are assigned at 100% of their effort. *See also* "Setting assignment units" later in this part.

Typically, you assign resources at the subtask level. However, you can assign resources to summary tasks if the resources are involved with all the subtasks or have some supervisory role over a family of tasks. In such cases, you track the resource's activity at the summary task level. *See also* Part III for information on outline levels.

If you're using the Assign Resources dialog box and decide you want to assign a resource you haven't created yet, you can do so by typing the resource name in a blank cell in the Name column. You can fill in the resource details later from the Resource Information dialog box, but the ability to create and assign new resources on the fly is a nice convenience. *See also* Part V for more information about creating resources.

Setting assignment units

In addition to assigning an existing or new resource to a task, you also need to set the assignment unit, which is the percentage of time that a resource works on a task. When you create a resource, you specify a resource calendar that defines the resource workday and workweek. The assignment-unit percentage is based on that working calendar. So if a person works a 40-hour week, assigning that resource to a task at 50% of units will have him or her working 20 hours a week throughout the life of the task. The default assignment is 100%.

When you create a resource, you set a maximum unit, which is the maximum percentage of work that a resource can put in on a task without being overallocated. If you assign a resource to multiple tasks within the same timeframe so that the resource exceeds those maximum units, Microsoft Project displays a resource overallocation icon in the Indicators column. *See also* Part V for more about resource calendars and maximum units.

To set assignment units for a resource, follow these steps:

1. Click the Gantt Chart icon in the View bar along the left side of the Project screen. The Gantt Chart view appears.

2. Click a task name.

 3. Click the Assign Resources button on the toolbar. The Assign Resources dialog box appears.

4. In the Units column, click in the row of the resource you want to assign.

5. In the Units column, use the up and down spinner arrows to increase or decrease assignment units for the resource. For work resources, the assignment unit is a percentage of the resource's total effort. For material resources, the assignment unit is the number of units of material that you use, such as 10 cases of nails.

6. Click OK.

You can assign resources to work more than 100 percent, if you know they're going to work overtime on a particular task. Microsoft Project alerts you to a resource overallocation, but if you have a rationale for making the assignment, you can ignore the message. Material resources cannot be overallocated.

For more information about resource assignments, see *Microsoft Project 2000 For Dummies,* by Martin Doucette, published by IDG Books Worldwide, Inc.

Communicating Assignments to a Workgroup with TeamAssign

After you make task assignments, you need to tell your resources about their responsibilities. You can use the TeamAssign feature in Microsoft Project to send e-mail or Project Central messages to your resources. Resources can then accept or decline assignments by replying to your message. *See* "Accepting and Declining Assignments by E-Mail" earlier in this part and *see also* Part XIII for more about using Project Central.

Before your team members and you can use workgroup messages, you must install workgroup messaging.

Installing workgroup messaging

Microsoft Project provides a simple process for installing Workgroup Message Handler, the feature that enables workgroup messaging among your project team members.

To install Workgroup Message Handler, follow these steps:

1. Make sure Microsoft Project is closed and the Project CD is in your CD-ROM drive.

2. Double-click the My Computer icon on the Windows desktop to open Windows Explorer.

3. Double-click the CD-ROM drive icon. The Microsoft Project 2000 Setup window appears.

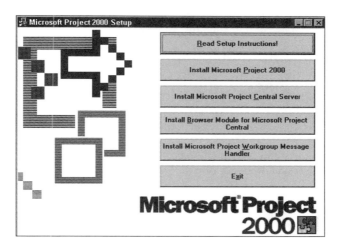

4. Click Install Microsoft Project Workgroup Message Handler. A window appears confirming the terms of installation.

5. Click Continue. The next Workgroup Message Handler Setup window appears.

6. Type your name and organization and then click Continue. The next Workgroup Message Handler Setup window appears, asking you to confirm the information you just entered.

7. Click Continue to confirm the information. The next window in the Workgroup Message Handler Setup sequence appears.

8. Change the destination for the Handler files or click OK to accept the default location. The next setup window appears.

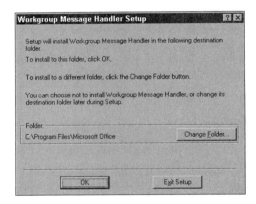

9. Click OK to initiate the setup. Microsoft Project checks disk space and installs the files.

10. When the final screen appears telling you the setup is complete, click OK to exit setup.

Sending a TeamAssign message

You can send TeamAssign messages for your entire project or for selected tasks only. When you send a TeamAssign message, all resources assigned to a task receive a message giving them the name of the task they're assigned to, the start and finish dates for the task, and the option of declining or accepting the assignment.

To send a TeamAssign message, follow these steps:

1. Click the Gantt Chart icon in the View bar along the left side of the Project screen. The Gantt Chart view appears.

2. If you want to send assignment information on certain tasks only, click to select the tasks.

3. Choose Tools⇨Workgroup⇨Team Assign. The Workgroup Mail dialog box appears.

4. Click the All Tasks or the Selected Task radio button to set which of these options Project should send messages to.

5. Click OK. The TeamAssign dialog box appears.

6. (Optional) In the Subject text box, you can change the subject of the message by typing new information.

7. In the To list box, verify that the resources are the ones you want to receive your message. If you don't want a particular resource to get your message, you can edit this field.

8. Click Send to send the TeamAssign message.

You cannot change any of the task information in the TeamAssign dialog box. If something in the Work, Start, or Finish columns needs to be changed before you send the message, click Cancel and make those changes in the Task Information dialog box.

 Tip: You can also send a TeamAssign message by displaying the Workgroup toolbar and clicking the TeamAssign button. *See also* Part XIII for more information about the Workgroup toolbar.

Project Timing and Resource Assignment

If you assign a resource to several tasks that take place simultaneously, you risk overallocating that resource. If an overallocation happens, Project places an icon in the Indicator column to alert you. You can see this overallocation a number of ways, such as in the Resource Usage and Histogram views. Assigning a resource too much work doesn't impact the timing of your tasks, however, unless you use Project's resource tools, such as leveling and contouring. These tools perform a series of calculations to make changes in your project to avoid these overallocations. If you use these calculations to get rid of resource overallocations, the trade-off is that Project may split or delay tasks to ensure that resources aren't working more than their maximum units.

 If the task you assign to a resource falls outside that resource's availability dates, Project doesn't stop you from making the assignment. It does, however, warn you of an overallocation.

Removing an Assignment

Sometimes you assign a resource to a task and then the resource declines the assignment. In other situations, you may decide after you're into the project that you want to replace one resource with another or that you don't need that resource on the task after all.

To remove a resource from an assignment, follow these steps:

1. Click the Gantt Chart icon in the View bar along the left side of the Project screen. The Gantt Chart view appears.

2. Choose View⇨Table⇨Entry. The Entry table appears in the spreadsheet area of the Gantt Chart view.

3. In the Resource Name column, click to highlight the resource for the task you want to modify and then press Backspace to delete the resource assignment.

Refining and Finalizing Your Project Plan

After you enter all your information in Microsoft Project, you still need to step back and take a good look at how that information affects your time and money. Having created perhaps hundreds of tasks and assigned dozens of task resources, you're bound to discover a few glitches. This part discusses the features that Microsoft Project gives you to identify and resolve potential problems before your project gets underway.

In this part . . .

Building in Slack

Slack is the amount of time a task can be delayed before that task becomes part of the critical path. The critical path consists of all tasks that have no slack; any delay in these tasks threatens the completion of the entire project. Microsoft Project enables you to manage slack in two ways:

✔ **Pad the schedule for individual tasks,** adding extra time when you first estimate each task's duration. In an ideal world, a task may take two weeks, but because things rarely go smoothly, you allow two and a half weeks. If you later need to remove some slack time, you can change the duration of individual tasks.

✔ **Create an individual task called Slack,** designating this task as the last task in your project and giving this task an appropriate duration — say, three weeks. As you modify your project to make your deadlines and resolve resource conflicts, you may see this task extend beyond your target finish date. If so, you can reduce the duration of this one task to make your project end on time, or you can change your project's finish date to make the timing more realistic.

Whichever method you prefer, be sure to build some slack time into your project. Tasks and projects slip, and the more time you build in to accommodate delays, the better off you're going to be when review time rolls around.

Filtering Information

Filtering allows you to highlight or display only the information that meets certain defined criteria, such as tasks that are on the critical path (the series of tasks that can't be delayed without delaying the final deadline of the project) or tasks that are running late or over budget. Microsoft Project's filtering feature is very sophisticated and offers you both built-in filters and the ability to create your own custom filters.

By turning on a filter, you can focus on information that helps you to identify problems with overworked resources, schedule timing, or over-budget tasks. Then, you can take action to resolve these problems before you finalize your plan.

Applying AutoFilter

AutoFilter is a set of predefined filters that are organized by types of project information. In any spreadsheet view, you can turn on the AutoFilter feature, which allows you to apply an AutoFilter from the drop-down menus on selected column headings. This ability to select the filters from your view makes them somewhat quicker and easier to use than the standard Filter feature. In addition, AutoFilter provides more project-specific filters; for example, an AutoFilter for filtering tasks by start date lists all the project's defined start dates so that you simply choose the one you want. With a non-AutoFilter filter, you have to edit the filter for a specific date — which is a much lengthier process than simply applying an AutoFilter.

To turn on the AutoFilter feature and apply a filter, follow these steps:

1. Display a view that contains a spreadsheet, such as the Gantt Chart or Resource Sheet view, by clicking that view's icon in the View bar along the left side of the Project screen.

 2. Click the AutoFilter button on the Formatting toolbar. Drop-down-list arrows appear in column headings where AutoFilter is available.

3. Click the arrow in any column heading that contains information of interest to you, and a drop-down list displays the filters related to that heading

4. Click a filter to apply it.

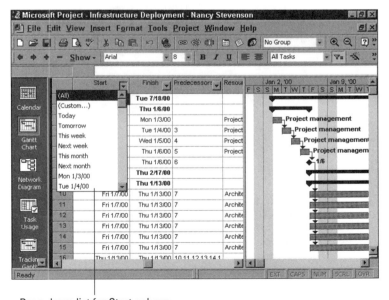

Drop-down list for Start column

Any tasks that don't meet the criteria of your selected filter disappear from view. To turn off all filtering, select All from any of the drop-down lists. To turn off the AutoFilter feature and hide the drop-down lists, click the AutoFilter button again.

If you apply both a normal filter and an AutoFilter, the normal filter applies first and then AutoFilter further limits the filtering.

Applying filters

In addition to using the AutoFilter feature, you can use a Filter feature that allows you to pick a filter name from a dialog box, edit that filter if you like, and then apply it. This process is a bit slower, but when you edit one of these filters, you can create multiple criteria that enable you to distinctly define a custom filter.

You can apply a filter in either of the following ways:

✔ Click the arrow beside All Tasks in the drop-down list box on the Formatting toolbar. Then select a filter to apply it. The drop-down list box assumes the name of the filter you select.

✔ Choose Project➪Filtered For and then select a filter from the side menu that appears.

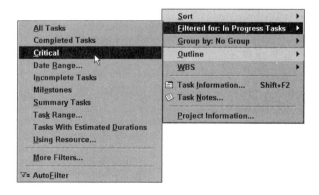

By default, filters remove items from your screen that don't match their criteria. You can change the action so that turning on a filter highlights items that match the criteria but leaves all other tasks on-screen so that you can view the filtered items in the context of your plan.

If you want to highlight rather than remove nonmatching items or if you want to see more filters than are listed in the Filter drop-down list or the Filtered For side menu, follow these steps:

1. Choose Project➪Filtered For➪More Filters. The More Filters dialog box appears.

2. Click the Task or Resource radio button to select the category of filters you want to view.

3. Use the scroll bar to locate the filter you want to apply.

   If you prefer to see the tasks that match the filter's criteria highlighted on-screen, click the Highlight button. If you want to remove from the screen any tasks that don't match the filter's criteria, click Apply.

If you select a filter that requires a value (Cost Greater Than, for example), a dialog box appears for you to enter that information.

Any on-screen filters that you apply also determine what information appears in a printout of your project.

Editing a filter

You can edit a filter to change the way that the criteria for a filter are handled by using a combination of four elements: And/Or, Field Name, Test, and Value(s).

To edit an existing filter, follow these steps:

1. Choose Project⇨Filtered For⇨More Filters from the menu bar. The More Filters dialog box appears.

2. Select the filter you want to edit from the list of filters.

3. Click Edit. In the Filter Definition dialog box that appears, you can click a button to insert a blank row or to cut, copy, paste, or delete selected rows. You can click in any blank row for any column to add more criteria, or you can click in a row under a column heading and use the drop-down list to select the following:

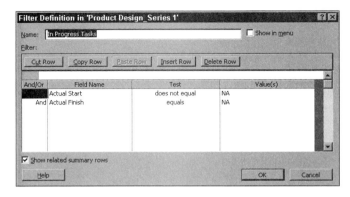

- **And/Or:** Means that both or only one of two defined criteria must be true.

- **Field Name:** Specifies the field that contains a value, such as Actual Start or Baseline Cost.

- **Test:** Checks for a specific condition when applying a filter, such as whether something is greater than, less than, or equal to something else.

- **Value(s):** Finds any absolute value(s) you may want to indicate. For example, if you want a filter for all tasks that cost $5,000, you type $5,000 here.

4. Click OK to save your changes.

 If you enter a value (baseline cost, for example) in the Value(s) column, the filter acts on all tasks relative to that value (say, all tasks that have a cost greater than the baseline cost). If you don't enter a value in the Value(s) column, Microsoft Project prompts you for a specific value whenever you apply the filter. Sometimes, entering a value each time you apply the filter makes more sense (for example, if you want to filter tasks that have a cost greater than a dollar amount that you choose when you apply the filter).

Creating a new filter

In addition to editing an existing filter, you can also create a new filter, which may be less confusing for you and others who are using your project than altering the built-in filters.

Creating a new filter is similar to editing a filter, except that you get to the Filter Definition dialog box differently. To create a new filter, follow these steps:

1. Choose Project⇨Filtered For⇨More Filters on the menu bar. The More Filters dialog box appears.

2. Click New. The Filter Definition dialog box appears.

3. In the Name field, type a name for the new filter.

4. Click to put a check in the Show In Menu check box if you want the new filter to appear in the menu.

5. Choose your criteria for And/Or, Field Name, Test, and Value(s).

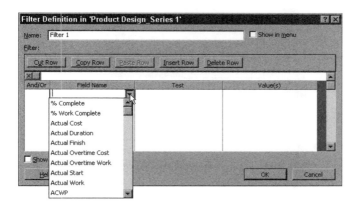

6. When you finish, click OK to save the new filter.

If you did not select the filter from the Filter drop-down list, you can access the filter by choosing Project⇨Filtered For⇨More Filters and then selecting it from the list in the More Filters dialog box.

Managing Costs

Before you finalize any Project plan, you should make sure the costs for task resources and fixed costs fit your project's budget. You can use Microsoft Project to analyze budget overruns and also to trim costs.

Reviewing project costs in Gantt Chart view

The Cost table in the Gantt Chart view is one of the best ways to see all your tasks' cost information. If you want to use this view to see your total project costs, be sure to create an upper-level summary task to which all other tasks are subordinate. The cost information for this upper-level summary task represents the total costs for your project.

To display the Cost table, follow these steps:

1. Click the Gantt Chart icon in the View bar along the left side of the Project screen. The Gantt Chart view appears.

2. Choose View⇨Table⇨Cost. The Cost table appears in the spreadsheet section of the Gantt Chart view.

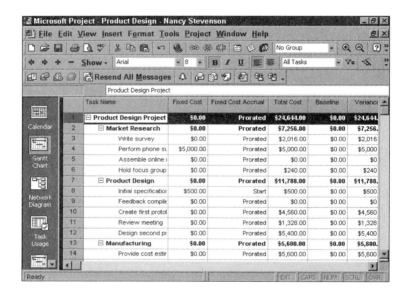

The most useful column to review initially is the Total Cost column. This column shows Microsoft Project's total calculated costs based on resource usage and fixed costs, which you can compare to any budget parameters you may have in mind for the project.

Reducing costs manually

If you're using a spreadsheet program (such as Excel) and you think a budget line item is high, you simply indicate a lower amount. In Microsoft Project, however, it's a little more complicated. You lower task costs by using any of the following methods, or a combination of them:

✔ **Reduce a task's duration.** If you estimate that a task will take three weeks to complete, consider reducing the completion time to save costs on resources.

✔ **Change the resource time on a task.** If you estimated that a resource will need to work full time on a task but after reviewing your assignments you feel that's not necessary, you can reduce that resource's percentage of assignment units. *See also* Part V for information on assignment units. Be sure, however, that any reduction in the percentage of assignment units is realistic and still allows the resource to complete the work.

✔ **Use fewer resources or less materials.** If a task can be accomplished in three weeks by using one resource, doing so will be cheaper than assigning two resources to a task for two weeks (which totals four weeks of resource time). If you can get by with ten gallons of paint instead of eleven, do so. If you have some time flexibility and think a task can be accomplished with fewer workers or less material, you can save yourself some money. However, if your original estimates were realistic, cutting these elements down is only a solution on paper. So, review all your project information carefully before making these kinds of changes.

✔ **Use cheaper resources.** Look around to see whether you have a similarly skilled resource with a lower per-use or per-hour rate. If so, delete the current resource assignment and assign the lower-priced resource. *See also* Part VII for information on assigning resources.

Monitoring Resource Workload

In addition to costs, you also need to check whether your resource assignments are realistic — is one person booked to work 23-hour days for a week or are management resources scheduled to work the week of the yearly management retreat? With Microsoft Project, you have several ways to review and resolve resource conflicts.

Resource Graph

The Resource Graph view displays a bar chart that shows you the total amount of effort a resource puts in on all the tasks in your project within a specific timeframe. You can display the Resource Graph view and modify the timescale to view a particular day, month, or quarter, for example.

To display and modify the timescale of a Resource Graph view, follow these steps:

1. Click the Resource Graph icon in the View bar along the left side of the Project screen. The Resource Graph view appears.

2. In the Resource Graph view, use the scroll bar at the bottom of the left-hand pane to move from resource to resource.

In the Resource Graph in the figure, Lin Chan is working 200% on the weeks starting December 19 and 26 — an overallocation shown by both the bar chart that exceeds the 100% allocation point and the percentages at the bottom of each bar.

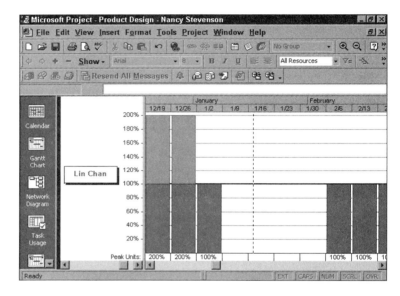

3. Use the scroll bar at the bottom of the right-hand pane to move forward or backward through time in your project.

You can change the timescale to view smaller or larger increments of time by following these steps:

1. Right-click anywhere in the timescale heading at the top of the bar chart. A shortcut menu appears.

2. Choose Timescale from the menu. The Timescale dialog box appears.

3. Choose any time increments you want (hours, days, weeks, months, and so on) in the Units fields for Major Scale and Minor Scale.

4. Click OK. The new timescale is displayed.

Resource Usage view

To review the specific hours that resources put in on individual tasks, you can display the Resource Usage view, which shows you each resource's assigned tasks, total hours per task, and days worked. By using the Resource Usage view, you can see what tasks are causing an overallocation and what their timeframes are. To review the Resource Usage view, click its icon in the View bar along the left side of the Project screen.

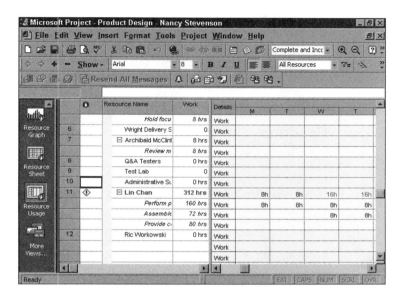

 You can also spot an overallocated resource by the exclamation point that appears in the Indicators column next to the Resource Name column in the Resource Usage or Resource Sheet views.

Resolving resource conflicts manually

After you check the Resource Chart and Resource Usage views to spot any resource overallocations (and before relying on Project's built-in resource-leveling calculations), you can try to resolve conflicts manually in one of the following ways:

✔ **Delete an assignment.** If a resource is simultaneously working two or more tasks, take the resource off of one assignment. You can then decide whether you need to replace that resource by assigning a different resource to the task.

✔ **Modify the assignment units.** If a resource can finish a task with a 50 percent effort, then change the assignment units to reflect that.

✔ **Lengthen a task.** Decide whether a resource can complete a task with a lower assignment-unit percentage if given more time.

  ✔ **Modify a dependency.** If no other resource can perform the tasks in conflict, you may need to create a dependency in which one task is completed before another task begins. By eliminating simultaneously occurring tasks, you eliminate the conflict. *See also* Part IV for more about dependencies.

  ✔ **Add other resources to an effort-driven task.** If a task's length is driven by the amount of resource effort expended, adding resources shortens the task, which may free an overallocated resource more quickly and eliminate a conflict with a later task.

  ✔ **Split a task.** If a portion of a task represents an overallocation, put the task on hold until the resource is free.

Resource Leveling

If you try everything and still can't solve your resource-allocation conflicts, then try using Project's Resource Leveling. Resource Leveling goes through a rather complex series of calculations based on factors — such as task priorities, task constraints, and available slack — that modify the timing of your scheduled tasks to eliminate resource conflicts.

Although Resource Leveling is a great feature that can solve your problems, it takes control out of your hands. For example, leveling may delay key tasks or split tasks that you prefer not to split, which is why you need to resolve conflicts manually, if possible, before using this feature.

For more information on resolving resource conflicts, check out *Microsoft Project 2000 Bible,* by Elaine Marmel, published by IDG Books Worldwide, Inc.

To use Resource Leveling, follow these steps:

  1. Choose Tools⇨Resource Leveling. The Resource Leveling dialog box appears.

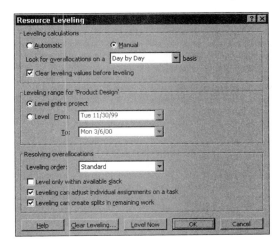

2. Click the Automatic radio button (if you want Project to apply leveling automatically when a resource conflict occurs) or click the Manual radio button (if you want to instigate the leveling each time by using the Level Now button).

3. Click to open the drop-down list in the Look For Overallocations field and select a time basis, such as Day by Day. If hourly overallocations are acceptable, but daily or weekly overallocations aren't, choose accordingly.

4. In the Leveling Range For Product Design section, click the Level Entire Project or the Level From and To radio buttons, select the start and finish dates by clicking the down arrows to open drop-down calendars, and then select dates.

5. In the Resolving Overallocations section, click the down arrow in the Leveling Order text box and then choose the leveling order from the drop-down list. You can level resources by selecting these options:

   • **ID Only:** Delays tasks with higher ID numbers before those with lower ID numbers

   • **Priority:** Sets tasks on a priority basis first and then applies other criteria, such as dependencies, slack, and so on

   • **Standard:** Sets tasks based on dependencies, slack, dates, task constraints, and task priorities

6. Limit the leveling by using these three options:

   • **Level Only Within Available Slack:** Allows Microsoft Project to use only available slack in its leveling calculations

- **Leveling Can Adjust Individual Assignments on a Task:**
  Allows Project to adjust a task to delay or split only a single
  resource and not all resources assigned to the task

- **Leveling Can Create Splits in Remaining Work:** Allows
  splits in tasks that are in process but currently unfinished

7. After you choose your settings, click Level Now to initiate the
   leveling calculation.

8. Click OK.

To see delays caused by Resource Leveling, display the Gantt Chart
view by clicking its icon in the View bar along the left side of the
Project screen. With the Gantt Chart view displayed, choose <u>V</u>iew⊅
Ta<u>b</u>le⊅<u>D</u>elay to display the Delay Table. This table includes a Leveling
Delay column that indicates how long leveling is delaying a task.

If you want to use leveling on a consistent basis, be sure to indicate
task priorities and any applicable constraints for every task so that
Microsoft Project has the full range of criteria to use in its calculations for prioritizing task delays in Resource Leveling.

Resource Contouring

New to Project 2000 is a feature called Resource Contouring, which
enables you to customize a resource assignment by designating
when a resource works the most hours. By default, a resource's
hours are evenly distributed over a task's duration. However, if you
have resource workload issues, you can weight your resource's
schedule more heavily at the beginning, middle, or end of a task, as
necessary.

To contour a resource's work on a task, follow these steps:

1. Click the Task Usage icon in the View bar along the left side of
   the Project screen. The Task Usage view appears.

2. Double-click the resource name under the task you want to
   modify. The Assignment Information dialog box appears.

3. Click the arrow on the Work Contour drop-down list box to display the contouring choices.

4. Click the option you prefer. Microsoft Project offers you the following choices:

   - **Flat:** The default contouring choice, which spreads the work
     evenly over the duration of the task.

   - **Front Loaded:** Schedules a resource to work more at the
     beginning of a task.

- **Early Peak:** Schedules peak work hours for the resource in the first half of the task.

- **Back Loaded:** Schedules a resource to work more at the end of a task.

- **Late Peak:** Schedules a resource to work peak hours in the second half of the task.

- **Double Peak:** Has a peak during the first half and a peak during the second half of the task.

- **Bell and Turtle (visually descriptive):** Works the resource the most in the middle of a task, as a bell or turtle's shape suggests!

5. Click OK to apply the resource-contouring choice that you make.

Reducing Total Time

Along with budget and resource allocation issues, you need to be aware of the total time it will take to complete your project. Often when you make modifications to deal with cost overruns and resource overwork, you lengthen your overall project. If doing so is acceptable, great. However, in many cases, finalizing your plan consists of a complicated orchestration of compromises regarding money, effort, and time.

Reviewing the critical path

The first step to understanding whether you have any extra time in your project plan is to examine the critical path. A critical path is the series of tasks that must be completed on time for you to meet your project deadline. Any tasks that aren't on the critical path have slack time, which is the period of time that they can run late without endangering your overall project deadline. By using slack wisely, you can reduce the time necessary to complete your project.

You can check your project's critical path in the following ways:

- ✔ Display the Gantt Chart or the Network Diagram view by clicking their respective icons in the View bar. Turn on the Critical Path Filter by clicking the Filter drop-down list on the toolbar and then selecting it from the filters listed there.

- ✔ Display the Detail Gantt view by clicking its icon in the View bar. Critical task bars are highlighted in red in this view.

 ✔ Click the GanttChartWizard tool to bring up the wizard. In the second window displayed in the wizard sequence, choose Critical path as the information you want to display.

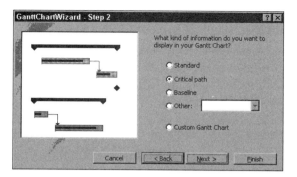

 You can also use the Grouping feature to group together tasks that meet certain criteria, such as tasks on the critical path or tasks that start later than a certain date. *See also* Part V for more about Grouping.

Methods for shortening projects

Project schedules are a complex interaction of task durations, dependencies, priorities, resource allocations, and Resource Leveling calculations — so trying to shorten your schedule can be complicated. As a project manager, you know the tasks that you can do quickly or when you can afford more resources. You have to make those decisions, but Microsoft Project offers the following methods to help you shorten your schedule after you do the following:

✔ **Assign more resources to effort-driven tasks.** If you think you can realistically obtain more resources, assign them to tasks to shorten your overall project-completion time.

✔ **Delete tasks.** Review your tasks for unnecessary work, such as a redundant inspection that you can eliminate.

✔ **Review durations.** Make sure your time estimates are accurate. At this point, you may be able to reclaim the slack time you built in for slippage when you first estimated the project.

✔ **Shift dependencies.** Assess whether, for example, you really have to wait for all the materials to arrive before you can begin to build your prototype. Then modify dependencies as you can to keep your project moving efficiently.

✔ **Adjust task constraints.** If you constrained a task to start or finish on a certain date, reevaluate the constraint and, if it's not necessary, remove the constraint to save time.

✔ **Clear Resource Leveling.** Because Resource Leveling delays or splits tasks, you can reverse Resource Leveling if it has thrown your schedule out of whack. You do so by making that choice in the Resource Leveling dialog box and then finding other ways to deal with resource conflicts.

Formatting Your Project

A typical Microsoft Project plan involves text and graphical representations of many elements — including tasks, indicators of progress, the critical path, the baseline, and so forth. Microsoft Project 2000 offers you almost overwhelming flexibility for formatting these elements. In this part, you discover several ways to show the information you need in the format you prefer.

In this part . . .

Choosing What to Display in a View

When you print your project for others to review, what you print is determined by what appears on-screen. You display a view by clicking that view's icon in the View bar along the left side of the Project screen. You can modify what you see in each view to show the information you want as clearly as possible.

If you haven't already done so, use the Spelling button to check for misspellings before you print.

Setting up a Project view

You can use the settings on the View tab of the Options dialog box to determine what appears in any Project view. To display the view options, follow these steps:

1. Choose Tools➪Options from the menu bar. The Options dialog box appears.

2. Click the View tab and set the following options:

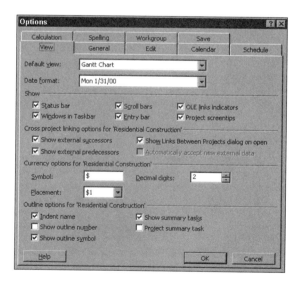

- **Default View:** Determines which view appears by default when you open any Project file.

- **Date Format:** Sets the format Project uses to display dates.

- **Show:** Displays screen elements, such as the Status bar and scroll bars.

- **Cross Project Linking Options for Project:** Determines what information Project displays about links to other projects (such as showing a marker on tasks that have external successors).

- **Currency Options for Project:** Sets the format that Project uses to display currency, including the monetary symbol and the number of decimal digits.

- **Outline Options for Project:** Determines the outline structure for your project. The options also include a Project Summary Task check box that you can use to create a project summary task (which I strongly recommend).

3. Click OK to save your changes.

Displaying text alongside taskbars

In the Gantt Chart view, you can choose to display text alongside taskbars. Doing so is especially helpful for reading large printouts, where many columns of spreadsheet information may separate the taskbars from their identifying information, making it difficult to read across the page. Putting the task name or the resource names near the taskbar makes reading a schedule easier. You can place text labels above, below, on either side, or inside a taskbar.

If you want to place text within a taskbar, choose a thicker shape for the middle of the bar. *See also* "Customizing a taskbar's shape, pattern, and color" later in this part.

To determine what text, if any, appears along with a taskbar, follow these steps:

1. Click the Gantt Chart icon in the View bar along the left side of the Project screen. The Gantt Chart view appears.

2. Click the task you want to modify.

3. Choose Format⇔Bar. The Format Bar dialog box appears.

4. Click the Bar Text tab.

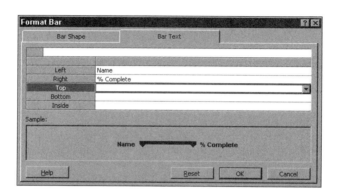

5. In the left column, click one of the five positions for text placement and, from the corresponding drop-down list, select the type of information you want Microsoft Project to display. The Sample area previews what your choices will look like.

6. After you make your selections, click OK to apply them.

Placing too much text around taskbars results in a cluttered chart, and the information becomes difficult to read. I recommend no more than three labels on any one taskbar.

To make changes to the text that's displayed around sets of taskbars rather than individual taskbars, you need to change the bar styles. *See also* "Formatting taskbar styles" later in this part for more information on bar styles.

Viewing dependency links

Microsoft Project enables you to choose whether to display lines between taskbars that represent dependency links. If you choose to display lines, you can choose what line style to use. To display dependency link lines, follow these steps:

1. Choose Format⇨Layout. The Layout dialog box appears. In the Links section, you can choose whether or not to display lines to represent dependency links as follows:

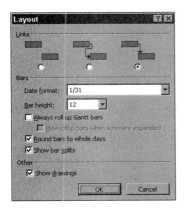

- **To display lines:** Click the middle or right radio button, depending on which of the two styles shown here you prefer.

- **Not to display lines:** Click the left radio button in the Links section of the dialog box.

2. Click OK to save any changes.

Customizing View Displays

In addition to the elements that you can modify in a Project view, you can also control certain parameters for the layout of those elements. For example, you can choose to show timeframes in a variety of scales, modify gridlines that mark those timescales, and adjust the size of rows and columns.

Modifying a timescale

The Gantt Chart view and a few other views, such as Tracking Gantt, have panes that display project timing with taskbars that are placed against a grid called a timescale. You graphically read the length of a task by observing where a taskbar falls in the timescale.

You can adjust the way the timescale indicates time increments and nonworking time, such as weekends. To modify the Gantt Chart timescale, follow these steps:

1. Click the Gantt Chart icon in the View bar along the left side of the Project screen. The Gantt Chart view appears.

2. Choose Format➪Timescale. The Timescale dialog box appears.

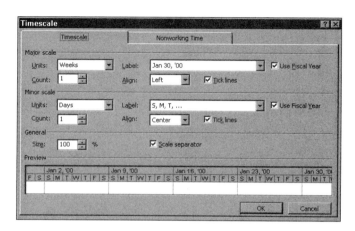

3. At the top of your project's taskbar section, two time increments appear. Click the Timescale tab and make any changes you want. Choosing larger time increments, such as quarters or years, gives you shorter taskbars but allows you to see a great deal of your project on-screen or in a report. Choosing smaller time increments, such as hours and days, lets you see more detail, but Project fits less of your plan on-screen and on each printed page. Choose from the following options:

   • **Major Scale.** The major timescale is the larger time increment and appears at the top.

   • **Minor Scale.** The minor timescale further breaks down the time increments that you see. The minor timescale falls directly below the major timescale.

   • **General.** The Size text box lets you use the up and down arrows to set the timescale's size (to fit more or less of the schedule on-screen). The Scale Separator check box lets you add or remove a check mark to specify whether you want a line to separate the major and minor scales.

In the Preview section, you can see how your changes affect the timescale format.

4. Click the Nonworking Time tab and, in the Formatting Options section, make any changes to the following options:

- **Draw:** The three radio buttons let you choose to display nonworking time in different ways: Behind the taskbars (so the taskbars seem to continue unbroken even during nonworking time), in front of the taskbars (so the taskbars seem to have breaks at points that are nonworking days, such as weekends), or not at all.

- **Color:** This drop-down list lets you choose a fill color for the taskbars.

- **Pattern:** This drop-down list lets you choose a pattern to fill the taskbars, such as horizontal or vertical stripes.

- **Calendar:** The drop-down list lets you choose on which calendar to base nonworking time. If you choose the 24 Hours calendar, for example, no time is marked as nonworking on the timescale. If you choose Standard, Saturdays and Sundays are marked as nonworking days automatically.

In the Preview section, you can see how your changes to the nonworking-time format affect your display.

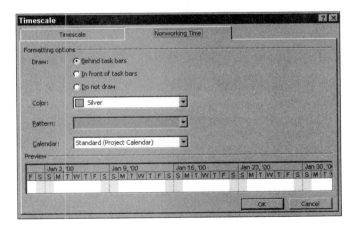

5. Click OK to save your changes.

You can also make changes to the timescale in the Calendar view. The settings are slightly different and do affect the calendar display itself. The calendar display resembles a desk calendar rather than a bar chart representation of time, as in the Gantt Chart view. Simply display the Calendar view by clicking its icon in the View bar and choosing Format⇨Timescale to see your options.

Modifying gridlines

To make reading your project easier, Microsoft Project can display several sets of gridlines. You can choose which gridlines to display and modify the gridline format.

To change the gridlines, follow these steps:

1. Display the view in which you want to modify the gridlines by clicking that view's icon in the View bar along the left side of the Project screen. Depending on the view you display, the gridlines that are available to change will vary slightly.

2. Choose Format⇨Gridlines. The Gridlines dialog box appears.

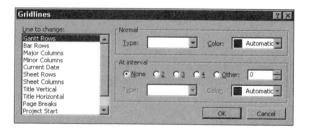

3. To change a set of gridlines, click the gridline name in the Line To Change list.

4. Adjust the gridline format by selecting a different style from the Type drop-down list and/or a different color from the Color drop-down list.

5. If you want the gridline appearance to change automatically at some preset interval, set the interval, the type, and the color of the gridline in the At Interval section of the Gridlines dialog box. For example, if you want to delineate every other row in the Gantt Chart with a red gridline, choose 2 for the interval. *Note:* The interval option is not available for all gridlines.

6. Click OK to save your changes.

Adjusting row height and column width

To accommodate a long string of text in the cells of a spreadsheet section of a view, you may need to adjust row height or column width. You can manipulate individual rows or columns by using the click and drag method. To do so, follow these steps:

1. Display the view you want to change by clicking that view's icon in the View bar along the left side of the Project screen.

2. Place the cursor on the side of a column or the bottom of a row that you want to resize. The cursor turns into a line with an arrow pointing up and down if you place it on a column, or left and right if you place it on a row.

3. Click the edge of the row or column and, holding down the mouse button, drag the cursor until the row or column is the size you want.

4. Release the mouse button, and the row or column resizes.

You can also change at one time the height of all rows in a view by following these steps:

1. Display the view you want to change by clicking that view's icon in the View bar along the left side of the Project screen.

2. Click the Select All button in the upper left corner of the spreadsheet. (Yes, it's a blank gray rectangle.)

3. Click the bottom edge of any row and, holding down the mouse button, drag to resize the row.

4. Release your mouse button, and all the rows resize to the same height.

Formatting Elements

You can format individual elements in your project (such as text, taskbars, and Network Diagram view boxes), and you can change the size, color, and shape of the elements. By changing elements, you can make a more attractive printout of your schedule and make the information in your plan more readable.

Formatting text

Formatting text to make it a different size, color, or font can help make your project more readable. You can also use text size and font to get more information on a page when printing your project.

In addition to formatting text styles for your entire view, or for limited categories of information within your view, you can also apply unique formatting to a single row of text. Just click the row, choose Format⇨Font, and adjust the formatting settings for that single item in the Font dialog box.

To format text, follow these steps:

1. Display the view in which you want to format text styles by clicking that view's icon in the View bar along the left side of the Project screen.

2. Choose Format⇨Text Styles. The Text Styles dialog box appears.

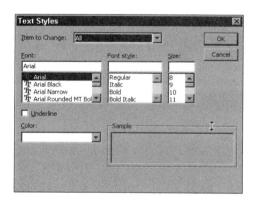

3. Click the Item To Change drop-down list and select the information category you want to format. If you want to format all the text in the open view, select All in this list.

4. Make any changes to Font, Font Style, Size, Color, and the Underline feature in the Text Styles dialog box.

5. After you make your choices, click OK to apply them.

As with any document, avoid going overboard with your formatting. Too many colors, a too elaborate font, or too many effects (such as italics or bold) can make your project difficult to read. Use text formatting for clarity and emphasis only.

Customizing hyperlink appearance

You can modify the colors used to indicate hyperlinks in your schedule. Although there is no practical purpose for this, if you prefer purple links to blue, Project gives you that flexibility. To modify hyperlink appearance, follow these steps:

1. Choose Tools⇨Options. The Options dialog box appears.

2. Click the Edit tab.

3. In the drop-down list in the Hyperlink Color field, click the color you want to apply to an unused link.

4. In the drop-down list in the Followed Hyperlink Color field, click the color you want to apply to a used link. Be sure this color is different from the unused hyperlink so that you can differentiate between the two.

5. Click OK.

Customizing a taskbar's shape, pattern, and color

Taskbars are important graphical indicators of your project's timing. Microsoft Project gives you a combination of settings to customize a taskbar's shape, pattern, and color. To format a taskbar, follow these steps:

1. Click the Gantt Chart icon in the View bar along the left side of the Project screen. The Gantt Chart view appears.

2. Click the task you want to modify.

3. Choose Format⇨Bar. The Format Bar dialog box appears.

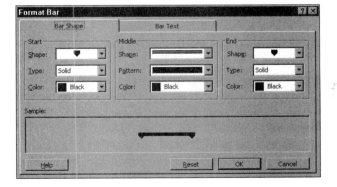

4. Click the Bar Shape tab.

5. Use the drop-down lists in the Start section to modify the graphical element that denotes the beginning of the taskbar. You can change the taskbar's shape, type (solid, dashed, or framed), and color.

6. Use the drop-down lists in the Middle section to make the taskbar's shape wider or thinner, to choose the bar's fill pattern, and to change the bar's fill color.

7. Use the drop-down lists in the End section to modify the graphical element that denotes the end of the taskbar by making choices like the ones you made in the Start section.

You can preview all changes to the taskbar in the Sample area.

8. Click OK to save your changes.

To format only a single, selected bar, use the Format Bar method just described in this section. To format the appearance of all your project's taskbars, use the method for formatting bar styles described in the "Formatting taskbar styles" section next in this part.

Formatting taskbar styles

If you want to change the appearance of an entire category of graphical symbols — all milestones or all summary tasks, for example — you do so by modifying bar styles. To change all taskbars of a specified type, follow these steps:

1. Choose Format➪Bar Styles. The Bar Styles dialog box appears.

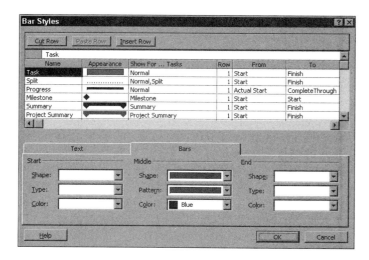

2. Click in the Appearance column for the taskbar element you want to modify.

3. Click the Bars tab.

4. Use the drop-down lists in the Start section to modify the graphical element that denotes the beginning of the taskbar. You can change the taskbar's shape, type (solid, dashed, or framed), and color.

5. Use the drop-down lists in the Middle section to make the taskbar's shape wider or thinner, to choose the bar's fill pattern, and to change the bar's fill color.

6. Use the drop-down lists in the End section to modify the graphical element that denotes the end of the taskbar by making choices like those you made in the Start section.

7. Click the Text tab.

8. Using the drop-down lists in each of these fields, select any text you want to appear alongside the taskbars.

9. Click OK to save your changes.

Although you can use the Bar Styles dialog box to change the criteria for each taskbar type, don't. You can get as confused about what each taskbar type represents as you would if you redefined each key on your keyboard and then tried to type a letter.

Formatting network diagram boxes

The Network Diagram view displays a unique graphical interface among Microsoft Project's views. In the Network Diagram view, task information appears in individual boxes with lines flowing among the boxes to graphically represent dependencies and the flow of work. You can format the border of each box, add color and pattern to the box's background, and format the text within the box to make the view more appealing to you or those who view your project. To format Network Diagram boxes, follow these steps:

1. Click the Network Diagram icon in the View bar along the left side of the Project screen. The Network Diagram view appears.

2. Choose Format⇨Box Styles. The Box Styles dialog box appears.

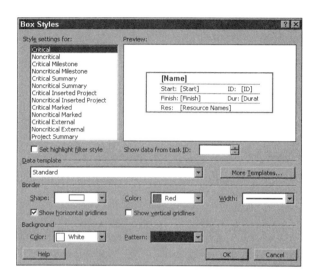

3. To format highlighted tasks, select the Set Highlight Filter Style check box; this toggles the function of this dialog box from formatting text to formatting filter highlight styles. Filters allow you to highlight on-screen or in printouts only the information that meets defined criteria, such as tasks over budget.

4. In the Style Settings For list, select the category of information for which you want to adjust formatting and change the following settings:

   • **Show Data from Task ID:** To display a particular task in the Preview section, use the up and down arrows to select the task by using its ID number, which is the number displayed along the left side of any spreadsheet view.

   • **Data Template:** To define what task information appears in Network Diagram boxes, select a template from the drop-down list or click More Templates for additional choices.

   • **Border:** To set the border shape, color, width, and gridline formatting, select the option you want in the drop-down lists and then click to select the check boxes to add or remove a check mark.

- **Background:** To set the fill color and pattern inside the Network Diagram boxes, select the Color and Pattern options you want from those drop-down lists.

5. Click OK to apply the changes.

Running the GanttChartWizard

The GanttChartWizard is a quick way to automate the formatting of your Gantt Chart view. In each of the Wizard's dialog boxes, you choose the information you want to display. Depending on your choices, the type and number of options may differ. However, after you make your choices, the GanttChartWizard applies all your formatting changes at once.

To run the GanttChartWizard, follow these steps:

1. Click the Gantt Chart icon in the View bar along the left side of the Project screen. The Gantt Chart view appears.

2. Choose Format⇨GanttChartWizard. A welcome screen appears.

3. Click Next to begin the GanttChartWizard sequence of dialog boxes.

   Your first option is to choose the information you want to display in the Gantt Chart view. Depending on your choices, other dialog boxes appear. To move forward through the dialog boxes, click the Next button. To move backward through the dialog boxes, click the Back button. To cancel the wizard at any time, click Cancel.

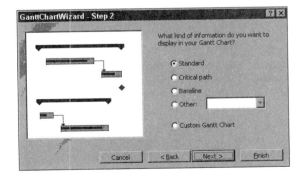

4. After you complete your settings, click Finish.

Saving Your Baseline and Protecting Your Project

You may spend days or months getting your Microsoft Project plan to a workable point, depending on the size and complexity of the project. However long you take to get there, you eventually know that your project is a go and that your plan is ready to distribute and implement. In this part you find out how to set a baseline and protect your project from prying eyes and unwanted changes.

In this part . . .

Baselines

A baseline is like a picture of your finalized plan and serves as a benchmark for tracking your project's progress. Baseline information includes all dates and costs associated with your project.

A baseline in a project is similar to a baseline in a scientific experiment: It's the rule against which you measure variations. This baseline function suggests a permanent record of your original plan, which you theoretically should never alter if you want a true record of your original estimates versus actual activity. However, major shifts sometimes occur in the focus, timeframe, or budget of a project. If that happens, you may want to reset the baseline, replacing your original estimates with completely new estimates, and tracking actual activity against that new baseline.

One option to replacing the baseline is to save interim versions of your plan's start/finish dates and display them alongside your baseline plan at any time. Doing this preserves your original plan, but also saves up to ten versions of modified plans that more accurately reflect your revised estimates at various points in the project.

Saving a baseline

When your project plan is ready, you can easily save a baseline by following these steps:

1. Choose Tools➪Tracking➪Save Baseline. The Save Baseline dialog box appears.

2. Click to select the Save Baseline radio button.

3. Click OK.

If you want to save a baseline for certain project tasks only, display the Gantt Chart view by clicking its icon in the View bar, and then click to select one or more tasks before you open the Save Baseline dialog box. In the dialog box, click to select the Selected Tasks radio button rather than the Entire Project radio button.

Resetting the baseline

You can reset the baseline at any time, which you may want to do because of a significant shift in project focus, timing, or budget that makes the previous baseline information irrelevant and, therefore, not worth tracking progress against. For example, if your project goes on hold for six months and then starts up again, every task in your baseline will appear to be grossly overbudget, and every task will be late.

Keep in mind, however, that resetting a baseline overwrites your original plan with all the current date and cost information you've entered to this point. Be aware, also, that you can set only one baseline. Resetting a baseline overwrites what you saved before. Either be very sure you don't need a record of that information before resetting, or save a version of the project file with that baseline before you reset if you do need to record that baseline for historical purposes.

To reset a baseline, simply choose Tools➪Tracking➪Save Baseline to save all current cost and timing information as the new baseline and to override the original.

Saving an interim plan

To help you monitor the many date changes that can occur in the life of a project, you may want to save interim versions of your plan. You can save up to ten interim plans. An interim plan saves only the actual start and finish dates for your project's tasks, along with baseline estimates of dates for tasks that have no actual activity recorded as yet. An interim plan does not save cost information. Especially in lengthier projects in which baseline information, though valuable to retain, becomes somewhat obsolete, you may want to save several interim plans along with the baseline. Doing this is a way of entering revised estimates without overwriting the original baseline plan.

You can save only one baseline in a Project file, so if you want to save several complete versions of your plan rather than only the start and finish information of an interim plan, simply save your project under another name and then reset the baseline. This approach preserves two or more complete versions of your plan without losing any information.

To save an interim plan, follow these steps:

1. Choose Tools➪Tracking➪Save Baseline. The Save Baseline dialog box appears.

2. Click to select the Save Interim Plan radio button.

3. In the drop-down list in the Into text box, select an interim plan start/finish number (anything from 1 to 10). You can save up to ten interim plans, and the choice you make here simply identifies the version you're creating.

4. Click OK.

Because you're limited to ten interim plans, if you subsequently want to use one or more of those slots for a more current interim plan, you can clear a saved interim plan and then save a new one with that number. Or, if an interim plan becomes obsolete, you may want to remove that information from your Project file. To clear an interim plan, follow these steps:

1. Choose Tools➪Tracking➪Clear Baseline. The Clear Baseline dialog box appears.

2. Select Clear Interim Plan and then select from the drop-down list the name of the plan you want to clear.

After you save your interim plans, you can display their start/finish dates by right-clicking the column heading in the Gantt Chart view. Select Insert Column from the shortcut menu and then select the Start/Finish column labeled with the interim plan number that you want to display.

Clearing the baseline

If you need to return to the planning stage of your project and remove baseline information entirely, or if your project parameters change so drastically that the current baseline information is obsolete, you can clear the baseline by following these steps:

1. Choose Tools➪Tracking➪Clear Baseline. The Clear Baseline dialog box appears.

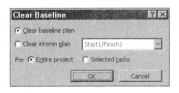

2. Click to select the Clear Baseline Plan and the Entire Project radio buttons.

3. Click OK.

Protecting Your Project

Project files are often shared among many people, from the project manager to management to project team members and even to clients or vendors. Protecting your plan from the possibility of unwanted changes is always a good idea, and Project offers several ways of doing so.

Making a file Read-Only

You can use Microsoft Windows file attributes to designate a file as Read-Only, which simply means that a file can be opened and viewed but not changed. Doing this is useful when you want to distribute a project file but you don't want to risk having somebody make changes to your file with information you haven't reviewed and then forward the file to others. To make a file Read-Only, follow these steps:

1. From the Windows desktop, choose Start⇨Find⇨Files or Folders. The Find All dialog box appears.

2. Right-click the Microsoft Project filename that you want to make Read-Only.

3. From the shortcut menu that appears, choose Properties. The Properties dialog box appears.

4. Click the Read-Only check box.

5. Click OK.

Protecting with passwords

Microsoft Project also offers you some security with its password feature. Password protection comes in these two basic variations:

✔ **Protection Password:** Means that no one can open the file for any reason without entering the correct password.

✔ **Write Reservation Password:** Prompts users for the password when they open the project file. Users who don't know the password can look at the file but can't save any changes to it.

You can apply both a Protection Password and a Write Reservation Password, ensuring both kinds of protection for your file.

To create a password for your file, follow these steps:

1. Choose File⇨Save As. The Save As dialog box appears.

2. Click the Tools menu at the top of the dialog box and select Save Options. The Save Options dialog box appears.

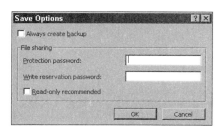

3. Type a password in one or both fields.

4. Click OK.

 You can set your file to display a message whenever it's opened that recommends the file be used as Read-Only by selecting the Read-Only Recommended check box in the Save Options dialog box. However, if you haven't applied password protection, doing this won't actually stop users from making changes — but they are warned not to.

Setting Project Central for online security

Project Central, the companion product that enables workgroup interaction online, has its own security features for files you post online for others to use. The person designated as administrator of the Project Central account controls not only who can create an account but also the authentication of users when they log on. The project manager for an individual project controls the frequency with which people can update a project file. *See also* Part XIII and the Appendix to discover more about these Project Central settings.

Setting macro virus protection

Macros are likely nesting places for viruses, so Microsoft Project alerts you when you run a macro that you didn't actually create. You can control the level of security that's associated with external macros that you run in your Project file by adjusting the security to low, medium, or high. With low security, all macros run; with medium security, you're warned whenever an external macro is about to run; and with high security, only macros from those you designate as trusted sources run.

Choosing low-level macro protection is not a good idea — but if you want to use low-level protection for some reason, be sure you install and use good antivirus software to catch potential macro viruses before they hit your Microsoft Project file.

To set macro virus protection, follow these steps:

1. Choose Tools⇨Macro⇨Security. The Macro Security dialog box appears.

2. Select the low, medium, or high setting.

   If you select a high setting, you also click the Trusted Sources tab and type the names of your trusted sources.

3. Click OK.

Monitoring Project Activity

One truism about projects is that they don't stand still. As work progresses on your carefully planned tasks, delays occur, people drop out, contracts get held up, and mission statements are rewritten. To help you deal with all that can happen to your project, Microsoft Project gives you several features for updating, tracking, and adjusting your data. Using Project's tracking features is key to turning Project into more than just an expensive to-do list maker. In this part you find out how to enter information about actual activity on your project and how to view your progress.

In this part . . .

Adding New Tasks to Your Baseline

Tracking your project is not only for keeping on top of task activity but also for revising estimates for tasks that are incomplete or haven't even started. To help you keep your schedule current, you can add new tasks to your baseline. *See also* Part X for information about setting interim plans.

You can add new tasks to the baseline by following these steps:

1. Click the Gantt Chart icon in the View bar along the left side of the Project screen. The Gantt Chart view appears.

2. Select the task or tasks you want to add to the baseline.

3. Choose Tools⇨Tracking⇨Save Baseline. The Save Baseline dialog box appears.

4. Click the Selected Tasks radio button.

5. Click the Save Baseline radio button.

6. Click OK.

The task or tasks are saved as part of your original baseline.

Be very careful to choose Selected Tasks when you reset the baseline to add new tasks. If you mistakenly select Entire Project, you overwrite the entire original baseline when you accept the changes.

Automating Updates

In Microsoft Project, you can update task information in several ways. Two tracking tools, which are called Update Tasks and Update Project, allow you to automate the updating process and record several pieces of tracking information at one time by entering that information in their respective dialog boxes.

To use any of the tracking methods discussed in this chapter, you must first set a baseline for your project. *See also* Part X for more information on setting a baseline.

Update Tasks

Update Tasks is a feature of Microsoft Project that puts in one place all the task information that requires updating, which makes tracking quicker. To use the Update Tasks feature, follow these steps:

1. Click the Gantt Chart icon in the View bar along the left side of the Project screen. The Gantt Chart view appears.

2. Click to select the task you want to update.

3. Choose Tools⇨Tracking⇨Update Tasks. The Update Tasks dialog box appears, including the following options for tracking task activity:

   - **Duration:** Represents the total of the actual duration to date plus any remaining estimated duration. If a task is marked as complete, with start and finish dates filled in, the duration is the actual duration of the completed task.

   - **% Complete:** Indicates the amount of work performed on a task, such as 50% for a task that is halfway done, or 100% if the task is finished.

   - **Actual Duration (Actual Dur):** Displays the amount of time a task has taken to date. If the amount is the same as the baseline total duration, Microsoft Project considers the task complete. If the amount is shorter than the baseline total duration, Project looks at the baseline start date and assumes a certain number of days remain to complete the task. If the amount is longer than the baseline, Project looks at the baseline start date and assumes that the task is complete but exceeded the baseline finish date. *See also* Part X for more information on baselines.

   - **Remaining Duration (Remaining Dur):** Shows the amount of time left to complete a task. Microsoft Project uses this figure to calculate the Actual Duration and % Complete. For example, a 10-day task in your baseline plan that has 3 days remaining sets Actual Duration to 7 days and % Complete to 70%. The same 10-day task with 0 days remaining sets % Complete to 100%. If Remaining Duration exceeds the task's baseline estimate, Project assumes an estimate change for the task and adjusts the % Complete accordingly.

   - **Actual Start and Finish dates:** Indicate the dates a task begins and ends. You can enter the start date when the task begins and the finish date when the task is completed, or you can enter both dates when the task is completed. After you provide the finish date, Project automatically calculates % Complete, Actual Duration, and Remaining Duration.

   - **Current Start and Finish dates:** Represent the current dates that Microsoft Project projects, based on % Complete and Remaining Duration information. When you set the Actual Finish date, the Current Finish date changes to match the Actual Finish date.

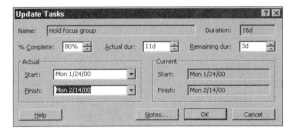

4. Complete the appropriate fields.

5. (Optional) If you like, you can click the Notes button and add a note, which will be saved in the Notes tab of the Task Information dialog box associated with the task.

6. Click OK after you make all your updates.

Update Project

Update Project helps you make sweeping updates to your project. For example, if a project started a month ago but you haven't recorded any activity yet, you can quickly track your progress by using the Update Project dialog box. This works best, provided a majority of the tasks took place on schedule and only a few need to be rescheduled.

To use Update Project, follow these steps:

1. Click the Gantt Chart icon in the View bar along the left side of the Project screen. The Gantt Chart view appears.

2. If you want to use the Update Project feature only for some tasks, select those tasks. If you want to use this feature for your entire project, you do not need to select any tasks.

3. Choose Tools➪Tracking➪Update Project. The Update Project dialog box appears, with the following options:

   • **Update Work as Complete Through:** Updates your project through the date specified in the drop-down calendar (which is set at today's date by default).

   • **Set 0% - 100% Complete:** Enables Project to calculate the percent complete for each task, assuming the tasks start and progress on time.

- **Set 0% - 100% Complete Only:** Tells Project to set at 100% any tasks that should be complete according to the baseline and to leave any uncompleted tasks at 0% .

- **Reschedule Uncompleted Work to Start After:** Reschedules any unfinished tasks to begin after the date you select in the drop-down calendar.

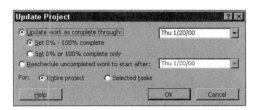

4. Select a method for updating work.

5. Set the way you want Microsoft Project to apply your settings by selecting either the Entire Project or the Selected Tasks radio button.

6. Click OK to update your project.

Recording Progress on Tasks

You can update your tasks' progress by using the Tracking toolbar, entering progress in Task Information dialog boxes, or completing information in columns in several Microsoft Project views. No matter how you record a project's progress, you need to include the following information:

✔ Percent complete

✔ Actual start and finish dates

✔ Actual duration

✔ Remaining duration

Updating with the Tracking toolbar

One of the quickest ways to track a tasks' progress is to use the tools on the Tracking toolbar. To display the Tracking toolbar, choose View⊅Toolbars⊅Tracking.

Project Statistics   Update Tasks

Reschedule Work

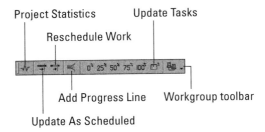

Add Progress Line   Workgroup toolbar

Update As Scheduled

The tools on the Tracking toolbar help you record and monitor progress on selected task as follows:

✔ **Project Statistics:** Opens the Project Statistics dialog box to display the overall project's start and finish dates, plus the work and costs for the entire project.

✔ **Update As Scheduled:** Updates a task by recording activity according to the baseline as of the current date. For example, suppose your project includes a task that starts on 3/10 and takes 4 days. If you click this tool on 3/20, you get a record that indicates the task started on 3/10 and finished on 3/14, in compliance with your baseline.

✔ **Reschedule Work:** Starts all remaining task work on a status date that you set in the Project Information dialog box or on the current date. To set a task date in the Project Information dialog box, choose Project⇨Project Information in the menu bar.

✔ **Add Progress Line:** Changes your mouse cursor into a jagged line so you can move the cursor over the timescale in your Gantt Chart view and click the spot where you want a progress line to appear.

✔ **0% - 100% Tools:** Allow you to quickly mark % Complete on a task.

✔ **Update Tasks:** Displays the Update Tasks dialog box for the selected task. *See* the "Update Tasks" section earlier in this part for a detailed explanation of the settings in that dialog box.

✔ **Workgroup toolbar:** Displays the Workgroup toolbar, which has several tools to help you communicate with your project team. *See also* Part XIII for more about communicating with workgroups.

The Status Date drop-down list in the Project Information dialog box allows you to update the status of your project as of a particular date, which may not be the present date. For example, if today is Tuesday and you want to update tasks as of last Friday, you can do so. Project uses your selected Status Date to calculate earned value (or the value of work completed) and to set progress lines to the date you specify. If the Status Date field reads NA, Project uses the current date as the status date.

Recording percent complete

Your calculation of how much of a task is finished constitutes % Complete. This percent can be quantitative (such as a manufacturing task with 75% of the products complete) or qualitative (your estimate that a task is about halfway done).

Sometimes you can calculate the percentage of a task that is complete based on the number of resource hours worked. For example, if a task assignment requires ten hours of quality assurance testing on a product, usually the task is half done after five hours. At other times, however, you may find that the effort you thought necessary to finish a task only partially completes the task.

Using the tools on the Tracking toolbar is your quickest method if you want to track the percentage of a task that's complete in 25, 50, 75, or 100 percent increments. However, if you want to record some other increment of % Complete, the best view to use for performing updates is the Task Details Form.

To record the % Complete in the Task Details Form, follow these steps:

1. Scroll down the View bar along the left side of the Project screen and click More Views. The More Views dialog box appears.

2. Click the Task Details Form in the list of views.

3. Click Apply to display the form.

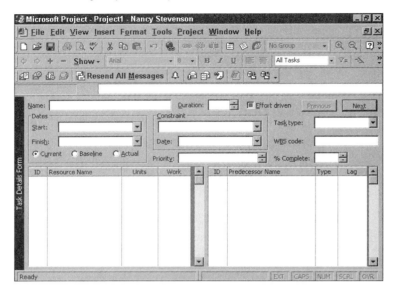

4. Click the Next or Previous button to move ahead or back to the task you want to update.

5. Use the up and down arrows in the % Complete field to enter a percentage. After you enter any information in this view, the Previous button changes to OK.

6. Click OK to save your information.

Entering actual start and finish dates

You can use the Task Details Form view to enter actual start and finish dates for tasks. For some tasks you enter an actual start date but don't enter the finish date until later. On shorter tasks (or if you procrastinate with your tracking), you may record the actual start and finish dates at the same time.

In addition to the Task Details Form view, you can denote the actual start and finish dates in several places, including the Update Tasks dialog box and any view that contains a spreadsheet with start and finish date columns, such as the Tracking Gantt view or the Gantt Chart view with the Tracking Table displayed.

To enter actual start and finish dates in the Task Details Form view, follow these steps:

1. Click the Task Details Form icon in the View bar along the left side of the Project screen. The Task Details Form view appears.

2. Click the Previous or Next buttons to locate the task you want to update.

3. Click the Actual radio button in the Dates section.

4. Click the Start field arrow and in the drop-down calendar that appears, select the actual date you started this task.

5. Click the Finish field arrow and in the drop-down calendar that appears, select the date your task ended.

6. Click OK to accept your entries.

If you enter an actual finish date without an actual start date, Microsoft Project calculates the start date based on task duration, even if doing so causes the start date to occur before the start of the baseline.

Specifying actual and remaining duration

Many tracking settings are interrelated. For example, if you specify the actual start and finish dates, Microsoft Project automatically calculates the actual duration. Likewise, if you enter the actual duration, Project automatically calculates when the task must have ended, based on the start date. If you prefer to specify duration rather than have Project calculate it based on other entries, you can do so after the task is completed or partway through a task, indicating how much work is completed and how much remains.

To enter the actual duration, follow these steps:

1. Click the Gantt Chart icon in the View bar along the left side of the Project screen. The Gantt Chart view appears.

2. Choose View⇨Table⇨Tracking. The Tracking Table is displayed in the spreadsheet section of the Gantt Chart view.

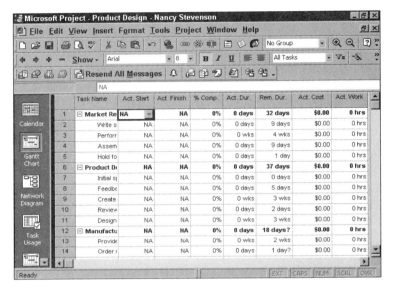

3. In the Actual Duration (Act Dur) column, click the task you want to update and then, using the arrows that appear, select a duration.

4. If the task will take more time to finish, click the Remaining Duration (Rem Dur) column and then, using the arrows that appear, select the remaining time.

Note: Microsoft Project calculates the % Complete based on how much time remains in the task. If you enter a % Complete and then an actual duration (or an actual duration plus a remaining duration) that's longer than the baseline duration, Project recalculates a new % Complete.

Recording Resource Activity

When you change a task's % Complete and Actual Duration, Project calculates the resource time and what that represents in costs, based on established resource rates.

The accrual methods you choose for resources and fixed costs impact whether costs accrue part way through the task, as soon as the task starts, or at the time the task is finished.

Remember: Just because a task requires a certain amount of time, not every resource will put in the same amount of time on that task. You need to enter the resource time that is actually spent on tasks to get accurate cost calculations.

Recording resource work

To record work performed by project resources, use the Resource Usage view, which is organized by the tasks to which a resource is assigned and provides columns that make it easy to update activity information.

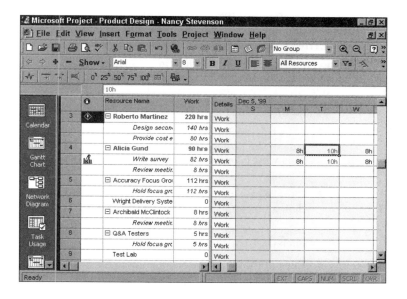

If you prefer to organize this resource information by tasks, with all the resources assigned to each task grouped together, use the Task Usage view by clicking the Task Usage icon in the View bar.

To enter in the Resource Usage view the amount of time a resource spends on a task, follow these steps:

1. Click the Resource Usage icon in the View bar along the left side of the Project screen. The Resource Usage view appears.

2. In the Resource Name column, find the resource you want.

3. In the right pane, use the scroll bars to locate the dates for which you want to record activity.

4. Click in the column for the day the resource performed the activity and enter the hours the resource worked. If the hours you enter differ from the baseline, the following things happen:

   • The Work column changes to recalculate total work for that resource on that task.

- The hours recorded on that date are highlighted in red, indicating a variance from baseline estimates.

- A symbol appears in the ID column, indicating that the assigned work has been edited.

See also Part XIII for information about resources using Project Central to report their task activity.

Entering overtime costs

Even if you enter more hours in a day than a resource is scheduled to work according to the resource calendar, Project doesn't apply overtime rates unless you tell it to.

To enter overtime for a resource, follow these steps:

1. Click the Resource Usage icon in the View bar along the left side of the Project screen. The Resource Usage view appears. This view is organized by resource, with all tasks to which the resource is assigned listed under it.

2. Choose Insert➪Column in the menu bar. The Insert Column dialog box appears.

3. Select Overtime Work from the list of available columns and click OK to display it.

4. Click in the Overtime Work column for the task and resource you want to update. Spinner arrows appear in the selected cell.

5. Use the arrows that appear to set the amount of overtime the resource works on the task.

Note: The overtime you set tells Project how many of the total recorded hours are charged at the overtime rate.

Using overtime shortens the duration of effort-driven tasks. Microsoft Project figures the work is getting done faster, because the resource is putting in more hours per day. If that's not the case, you may need to change the task to require more effort to complete it.

Viewing Progress

After you enter tracking information, you can see what actually transpires on your project and how that differs from your original estimates in terms of time and money. In addition, you can use progress lines for a snapshot of where you are on any given date in your project.

Viewing completed work on taskbars

When you track the progress of scheduled tasks, you can see that progress graphically represented in the Gantt Chart view or the Tracking Gantt view, as follows:

✔ Summary tasks indicate the progress of their subtasks with a segmented white bar displayed beside the baseline taskbar.

✔ Individual tasks display portions of their taskbars as solid to represent the completed part of the task. The percentage completed also appears by default next to the taskbar.

Summary task progress

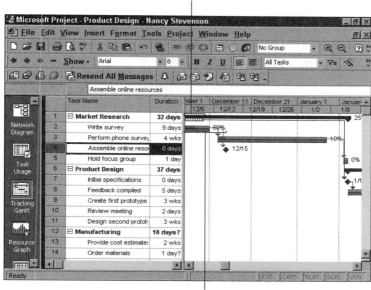

Task percent complete

You can modify the appearance of these graphical representations by choosing Format⇨Bar Styles from the menu bar.

Displaying time and cost variance

The Gantt Chart view has two tables that are particularly useful if you want to compare your actual activity to your baseline estimates. To use these tables, follow these steps:

1. Click the Gantt Chart icon in the View bar along the left side of the Project screen. The Gantt Chart view appears.

2. Choose View➪Table and select either the Variance or the Cost table from the side menu.

The Variance table lets you see how far behind (or ahead) you are in starting and finishing tasks. This table shows you Start and Finish dates that contain actual information for tasks with recorded activity, Baseline Start and Baseline Finish dates, and columns that show the variation between those sets of data.

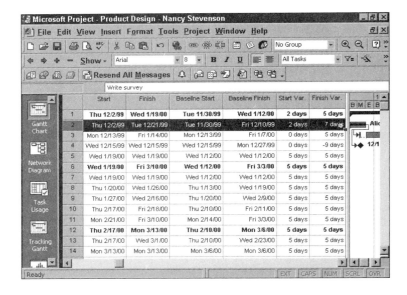

The Cost table makes clear (sometimes painfully) how far from your baseline budget you are in actual dollars spent. The columns of particular interest are

• **Total Cost:** Represents the total actual cost (according to activity tracked to date) plus remaining baseline costs.

• **Baseline:** Represents your original cost estimate.

• **Variance:** Indicates the difference between Total Cost and costs according to the Baseline.

• **Remaining:** Displays the amount of money left for any scheduled task work to be done.

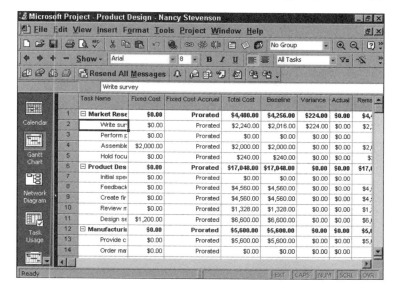

By studying these tables, as well as other tables and views, you get a good idea of whether you are straying in time or in money spent so that you can adjust your plan accordingly.

Displaying progress lines

Progress lines represent a snapshot of your project at the current date (as determined by your computer's clock) or the Status Date. (*See also* the "Updating with the Tracking toolbar" section earlier in this part for more information on the Status Date.) A progress line appears on the Gantt Chart as a vertical line that connects tasks currently in process with tasks that are late getting started. Doing this creates a zigzag line with peaks pointing to the right that indicate tasks that are ahead of plan and peaks pointing to the left that indicate tasks that are running behind.

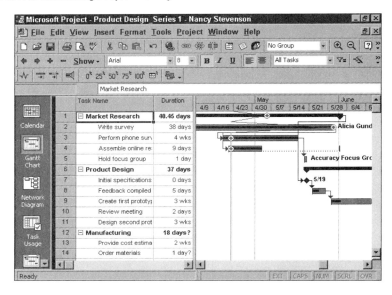

To display a Progress Line, follow these steps:

1. Click the Gantt Chart icon in the View bar along the left side of the Project screen. The Gantt Chart view appears.

2. Choose Tools⇨Tracking⇨Progress Lines. The Progress Lines dialog box appears.

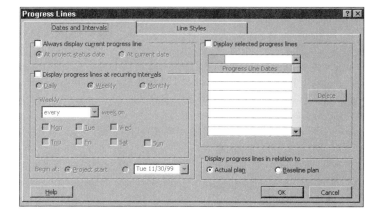

3. Click the Dates and Intervals tab.

4. If you want to see a progress line on-screen all the time, click to select the Always Display Current Progress Line check box and then select the At Project Status Date or the At Current Date radio button.

5. If you want progress lines to appear at regular intervals throughout your project, click the Display Progress Lines at Recurring Intervals check box and determine the interval time settings.

6. If you want to display a progress line for a particular date, click the Display Selected Progress Lines check box and either enter a date in a Progress Line Dates blank row or select a date from the drop-down calendar that appears when you click the Progress Line Dates list-box arrow.

7. If you want to show progress relative to the baseline, click to select the Baseline Plan radio button under the Display Progress Lines In Relation To section.

8. Click OK. The progress line appears in your Gantt Chart.

Reporting and Printing

With Microsoft Project 2000, you can easily generate a wide variety of sophisticated reports about your project. In fact, Project's reporting capability is one of its most powerful features, helping you keep your project team, management, and clients apprised of your progress. In this part, you discover the various report options that Project offers so that you can print and distribute the project information you want to communicate in an attractive format.

In this part . . .

Creating a New Report

In Microsoft Project, you can either create a new report or edit an existing one. You may decide to create your report from scratch because none of the predefined reports meets your information needs, or perhaps you have a standard company report that you use again and again and you don't want to edit an existing report each time you need it. To create a new report, follow these steps:

1. Choose View➪Reports. The Reports dialog box appears.

2. Click Custom to open the Custom Reports dialog box.

3. Click New. The Define New Report dialog box appears.

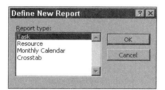

4. Select a report type and click OK. Depending on the report type you choose, the next dialog box that appears is labelled Resource Reports, Task Reports, Monthly Calendar Reports, or Crosstab Reports.

5. Type a name for your new report.

6. Click OK. Your new report name appears in the Custom Reports dialog box and is available to you anytime.

See "Editing an Existing Report" later in this part for information about the settings and choices that you can make to define your new report's contents.

 Name your reports descriptively so that others who work with them will understand their content. Rather than using MyReport1, for example, use something like Weekly Marketing Report for clarity.

Drawing with Project

By using the drawing feature in Project, you can direct a reader's attention to certain information in a report or include a sketch of a product or a process. You can create drawings in the chart pane of the Gantt Chart view by following these steps:

1. Click the Gantt Chart icon in the View bar along the left side of the Project screen. The Gantt Chart view appears.

2. Choose Insert➪Drawings. The Drawing toolbar appears.

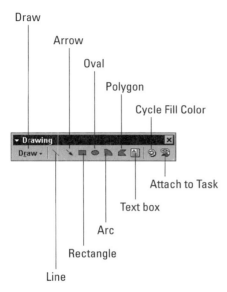

Draw

Arrow

Oval

Polygon

Cycle Fill Color

Attach to Task

Text box

Arc

Rectangle

Line

3. Click the drawing tool for the object you want to draw, such as a rectangle or a line.

4. Click the spot in the Gantt Chart where you want to draw the object and drag your mouse until the object is the correct size.

5. Release the mouse button.

6. (Optional) If the object you create is a Text box, click in it and type the text you want.

After you draw your object, you can use the Cycle Fill Color tool to color it. If you select an object and then click this button, Project fills the object with a color — just keep clicking and Project runs through a standard palette of colors, filling the object with one color right after the other. When you find the color you want, just stop clicking.

You can also use the nodes located around a selected object to resize it. Click the object, and the nodes appear. Click any node and drag it toward the center of the object to make it smaller or away from the center to enlarge it. When the object is the size and shape you want, release your mouse button.

TIP

A drawing normally stays wherever you put it on a page. However, if you want a drawing to always appear with a specific task, be sure to use the Attach to Task tool from the Drawing toolbar.

Editing an Existing Report

You can develop a report by customizing a preexisting report. This option is often easier than starting from scratch because there may already be a report that has some of the information you want to include. *See also* "Creating a New Report" earlier in this part.

When you edit a report, first you select a report to edit and then you edit slightly different information depending on the type of report that you select. Think of report types as the categories in which different reports fall. Reports have detailed editing settings that have slight variations based on whether the report deals with Task or Resource information or provides information in a Crosstab or a Monthly Calendar structure.

The initial steps for editing any report are the same, however. To edit an existing report, follow these steps:

1. Choose View⇨Reports. The Reports dialog box appears.

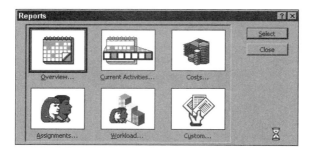

2. Click any report option and then click Select. Depending on the report selection you make (such as Custom, Costs, and so on), that dialog box appears.

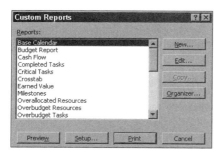

3. From the Reports list, select the report you want to edit.

4. Click Edit. The dialog box that appears depends on the type of report you plan to edit, such as a Task Report, Resource Report, Monthly Calendar Report, or Crosstab Report.

At this point, depending on the report type you choose to edit, you can choose from slightly different options.

A few reports don't take you to the dialog box as mentioned in the preceding steps. The Project Summary and Milestones reports only offer you the option of a text formatting dialog box when you choose to edit them. *See also* "Formatting Report Text" later in this part.

Editing a Task or Resource Report

When you select a report to edit that comes under the category of a task-type report or a resource-type report, a Task Reports or Resource Reports dialog box appears. The dialog box includes three tabs — Definition, Details, and Sort — in which you can change various report elements. Only the Definition tab offers slightly different choices for a task or a resource type of report.

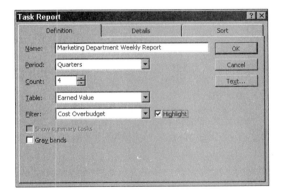

On the Definition tab, you can edit the following:

✔ **Name:** The name of the task you're editing.

✔ **Period:** The time covered, from a number of days to the entire length of the project.

✔ **Count:** The number of time periods to be included in the report.

✔ **Table:** The table on which you want to base the report contents. A table is a predefined set of columns of information that corresponds to the tables you can choose to display in a Gantt Chart view, such as a Costs or Entry table.

✔ **Filter:** Any filters you want to apply.

On the Details tab, you can edit the following:

✔ **Task/Resource**: Depending on whether you're working on a report that falls into the task type or the report type, this information varies slightly but includes, for example, the predecessor and successor for tasks, and the cost rate and calendar for resources. Simply click the check box for each piece of information you want to include in the report.

✔ **Assignment:** Offers four choices of information associated with either a task or a resource to include in the report, including Notes, Schedule, Costs, and Work. Simply click the check box for any piece of information you want to include in the report.

✔ **Border Around Details, Gridlines Between Details, and Show Totals:** Selecting one of these three choices automatically generates a border, gridlines, or totals of any cost information respectively.

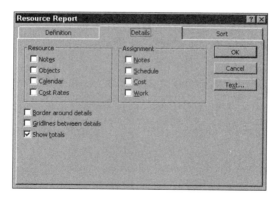

Although the first two tabs in the Reports dialog box deal with the content of a report, the third tab (Sort) deals with organizing content. For example, you can sort all tasks alphabetically. Because you can use the Sort feature with existing, new, and standard reports, it's covered in another section. *See* "Sorting Information in Reports" later in this part.

You customize a report by modifying any of these elements. When you finish your changes, click OK to save them.

Editing a Crosstab Report

Any report that falls into the Crosstab Report type, such as the Task Usage Report or the Who Does What When report, has a crosstab structure. A Crosstab Report looks at two types of information over a period of time — costs by task per week, for example. After you select a report that falls into the Crosstab Report type, click Edit. The Crosstab Report dialog box appears.

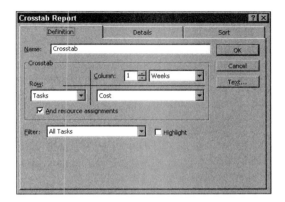

To set up a Crosstab Report, follow these steps on the Definition tab of the Crosstab Report dialog box:

1. In the Row text box, click the arrow to display the drop-down list and then select Tasks or Resources.

2. In the adjacent drop-down list, click to display the second piece of information for each row (for example, if you choose Tasks in the first drop-down list, you may choose Cost in the second). You have now selected the two pieces of information to be compared in the Crosstab Report.

3. In the Column fields, use the controls to set the time period and the number of periods to be shown in the report.

4. If you want, you can apply a filter so that the printed report shows or highlights only tasks that meet defined criteria, such as tasks on the critical path. When you apply a filter to a printed report, the text of highlighted tasks appears in color or bold, depending on your printer.

5. Click the Details tab and work through the following options:

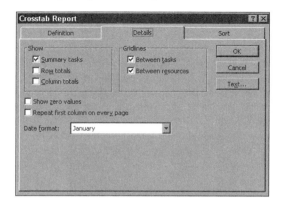

- **Show Summary Tasks:** Displays only summary level tasks.

- **Show Row Totals:** Displays total costs by row.

- **Show Column Totals:** Displays totals at the end of rows.

- **Gridlines Between Tasks and/or Between Resources:** Displays gridlines in your printed report.

- **Show Zero Values:** Puts a zero in a spreadsheet column that has no value.

- **Repeat First Column on Every Page:** Repeats the first column, which contains your first category of information, on every page of a multi-page report.

- **Date Format:** Shows the format you want to use for dates.

Formatting Report Text

In Microsoft Project, you can make all the formatting changes you're used to making to text in your favorite word processor program. You do so before you print a report.

To edit text format before generating a report, follow these steps:

1. Choose View⇨Reports from the menu bar. The Reports dialog box appears.

2. Click a report category and then click Select.

3. In the Reports dialog box, select the report you want to use.

4. Click Edit. At this point, one of two things happens:

   - The Text Styles dialog box appears. Some reports, such as Task Usage or Project Summary, only offer text formatting choices before printing.

- The Report dialog box appears. Click the button labeled Text. The Report Text dialog box appears.

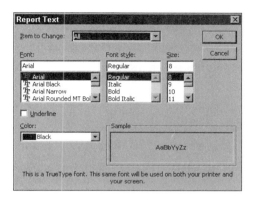

5. In the Item To Change drop-down list, select which items to format.

6. Select the Font, Font Style, Size, and Color. A preview of the font selection appears in the Sample box.

7. Click OK to save your settings.

Inserting Graphics

To generate attractive documents about your project, you may want to include a graphic, such as a company logo. To add graphics to project files, use the following options:

🖙 Cut and paste from another document.

🖙 Link to a graphics file (which keeps your project file smaller).

🖙 Embed a graphic, which allows you to edit its contents in Microsoft Project even though the graphic was created in another program, such as PowerPoint.

Project lets you add graphics only in the following places:

🖙 The chart section of the Gantt Chart view

🖙 Notes

🖙 Headers, footers, and legends (labels you can add to elements of a project when generating a printout).

Consider placing pictures of resources in resource notes, especially if you're dealing with a lot of people you just met and you want to remember what they look like. However, beware of expanding the size of your project file to accommodate too many graphic images.

To insert a graphic by using the object linking and embedding method in the Gantt Chart view, follow these steps:

1. Click the Gantt Chart icon in the View bar along the left side of the Project screen. The Gantt Chart view appears.

2. Choose Insert⇨Object. An Insert Object dialog box appears.

3. Select the type of object you want to insert.

4. Click OK.

A dialog box appears and, depending on the type of object you select, gives you a number of options, such as the Microsoft Clip Gallery or an Excel chart.

5. Make your choices for the specific object and click OK to place it in your document.

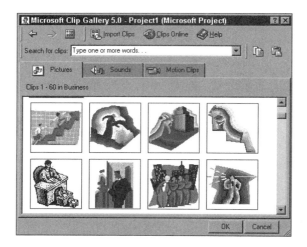

To insert a graphic in a header, footer, legend, or note, follow these steps:

1. Open the feature you want by choosing View⇨Header and Footer or double-clicking a task name in the Gantt Chart view and clicking the Notes tab in the Task Information dialog box.

2. Click the Insert Picture tool. The Insert Object dialog box appears.

3. Select the type of object you want to insert and click OK. Depending on what kind of object you select to insert, a corresponding dialog box appears.

4. Make appropriate choices in the object dialog box, then click OK to insert the object.

 For more information about drawing and adding graphics, see *Microsoft Project 2000 For Dummies,* by Martin Doucette (published by IDG Books Worldwide, Inc.).

Printing Reports and Projects

You can print any report or project. When you print a project, the printout reflects whatever view appears on-screen at the time you print. When you print a report or a project, you must set certain page-setup parameters (including the use of headers, footers, margins, and page orientation) in the Page Setup dialog box.

Setting margins

The ability to modify page margins enables you to determine the amount of information that fits on a page and to make your document more attractive.

To set margins, follow these steps:

1. Choose File⟹Page Setup. The Page Setup dialog box appears.

2. Click the Margins tab.

3. Click the arrows to set the Top, Right, Left, or Bottom margins to a higher or lower setting than the default.

4. (Optional) If you want to use a border to designate the margins around the page, click Every Page or Outer Pages in the Border section of the Margins tab.

5. Click OK to accept your settings.

 Don't make your margins too small. Too much information crammed on a page makes an unreadable document. If you need to fit more information on a page, consider modifying the column sizes in the Gantt Chart view or reducing text size in your report.

Setting up page output

Some basic page settings affect your printed document's page orientation, scaling of output, and paper size. These features, in turn, affect the amount of information printed on each page and the number of pages in your document.

To set these page features, complete the following steps:

 1. Choose File⇨Page Setup. The Page Setup dialog box appears.

 2. Click the Page tab and then set whichever of the following adjustments you want:

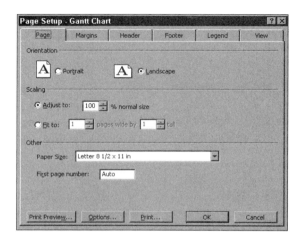

 • To set page orientation, select the Portrait or Landscape radio button.

 • To scale your output, select the Adjust To radio button to scale by a percentage or the Fit To radio button to establish the width and height of a page within which you want to fit your output.

 • To set paper size, select the size you prefer from the Paper Size drop-down list.

 3. Click OK to save the settings.

Adding a header or footer

Headers and footers come in handy for putting information (such as project name, contact information, page numbers, or the date and time a report is printed) into long reports. Although you decide whether to and what to include in a header or footer, you set up the features in the same way. In the Page Setup dialog box, separate Header and Footer tabs offer identical settings.

To add a header or footer, follow these steps:

 1. Choose File⇨Page Setup from the menu bar. The Page Setup dialog box appears.

2. Click the header or footer tab.

Insert Page Number

Insert Current Date

Insert File Name

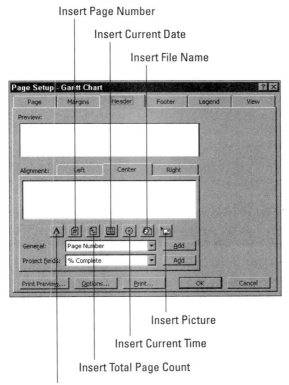

Insert Picture

Insert Current Time

Insert Total Page Count

Format Text Font

3. Click an Alignment tab (Left, Center, or Right) that represents where you want information to appear on the page. *Note:* You can place more than one piece of information (such as page number and date) in each of the three positions.

4. Type any text that you want to appear in your document's header or footer. As you enter information in the Alignment text box, a preview of how the text lays out on the printed page appears in the Preview box.

5. Use the General and the Project Fields drop-down lists to select project information that you want to include.

6. Click Add.

7. To add a picture or format text in the header or footer, click the Insert Picture or the Format Text Font buttons to do so. For more information about these features, *see also* "Formatting Report Text" and "Inserting Graphics" in this part.

8. Click OK after you add all the information you want in your header or footer.

If you want, you can use the tool buttons on the Header and Footer tabs as shortcuts to add automatic page numbering, total page count, current date, current time, or the filename. These tools are useful because they're dynamic, meaning they place the most current information in the document (such as today's date) rather than static text that you enter manually. Microsoft Project inserts current information every time you print the report, so you don't have to add updated information in the header or footer each time you print the document.

To start page numbering with a number other than 1, type the number you want in the First Page Number text box on the Page tab in the Page Setup dialog box.

Setting up a legend

A legend is a way of adding explanatory information to your printed document. When you print a report with a legend, the legend provides a key to any graphic symbols and objects in your report, as well as any other information you want to include.

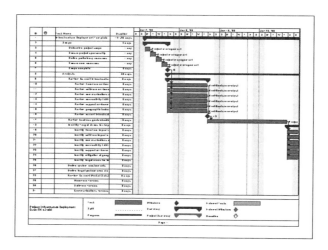

You set up legends in much the same way you set up headers and footers, with one exception. If you don't want headers and footers to appear on your pages, you simply don't put any information in them. However, if you don't want a legend to appear, you must change the default setting from Legend On Every Page to Legend On None. Otherwise, a legend defining any graphic elements automatically appears at the bottom of your pages.

To set up a legend, follow these steps:

1. Choose File⇨Page Setup. The Page Setup dialog box appears.

2. Click the Legend tab.

3. Click an Alignment tab (Left, Center, or Right) to indicate where you want information to appear on your page. *Note:* You can place more than one piece of information in each of the three positions if you want.

4. Type any text you want to appear in the legend. As you enter information in the Alignment text box, a preview of how the text lays out on the printed page appears in the Preview box.

   If you want, you can use the tool buttons on this tab as shortcuts for entering automatic page numbering, total page count, current date, current time, or the filename.

5. Use the General and the Project Field drop-down lists to select information that you want to include in the legend. Simply select your choice in either list and then click Add.

6. To add a picture or to format the text in the legend, click the Insert Picture or the Format Text Font buttons to do so. For more information about these features, *see also* the "Formatting Report Text" and "Inserting Graphics" sections in this part.

7. To format the labels that appear for defining graphic elements, click the Legend Labels button. The Font dialog box appears, allowing you to make standard text formatting settings, such as font, type size, and so on.

8. Click OK after you add all the information you need in your legend.

Print Preview

Being able to see what your report looks like before it's printed is often useful, especially for longer documents that use up a lot of paper if you have to print them again because of an error. You can get to the Print Preview feature in the following ways:

✔ In the Page Setup dialog box, click the Print Preview button on any of the tabs.

✔ After you generate a report, Microsoft Project automatically displays Print Preview when you open the report.

✔ Click the Print Preview tool on the Standard toolbar or choose File⌐Print Preview to see a print preview of whatever view is on your screen.

When the Print Preview appears, you can navigate the screen by using the following options at the top of the screen:

✔ Click the Page Left, Page Right, Page Up, and Page Down arrows to move around the report.

✔ Click the Zoom, One Page, or Multiple Pages tools to zoom in on the display or to adjust the number of pages showing on your screen at one time.

✔ Click Page Setup to make changes to your document output before printing it.

✔ Click Print to print the document.

✔ Click Close to close the preview without printing.

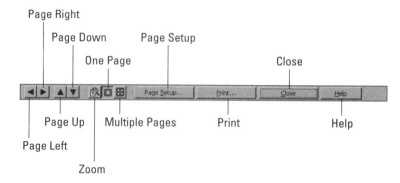

Selecting a Standard Report

In Microsoft Project, standard reports are predefined reports that offer a wide variety of content without your having to make changes or create a new report. With a standard report, all you do is select the report from a list of reports, format text any way you want it, and print the report.

To see the available standard reports and select one to print, follow these steps:

1. Choose View⇨Reports. The Reports dialog box appears.

2. Select any of the following five choices: Overview, Current Activities, Costs, Assignments, and Workload. A dialog box appears with the choices available in the selected category.

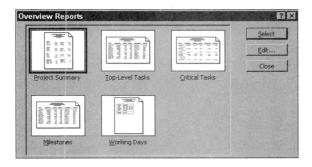

3. Click the report you want to generate.

4. Click Select. The report's Print Preview appears.

5. If the report looks the way you want it, click Print to print it. If the report isn't right, click Close to leave the preview so that you can make any necessary changes.

Sorting Information in Reports

When you generate a report, you have the option of editing it. One editing choice — sorting — allows you to organize information in your report according to three criteria. The first criterion takes precedence, then the second, and then the third. For example, if you sort first by Actual Cost Descending and second by Task Name, you get the highest-cost tasks first and the lowest-cost tasks last. If two tasks happen to have the same cost, the two are organized alphabetically by task name.

To set the sorting criteria, follow these steps:

1. Choose View⇨Reports from the menu bar. The Reports dialog box appears.

2. Click any of the reports listed, including Custom. The corresponding dialog box appears.

3. Click the Edit button. A dialog box appears, depending on the type of report you plan to edit.

4. Click the Sort tab.

5. Click the arrow in the Sort By text box. A drop-down list appears from which you select the type of information you first want to sort by.

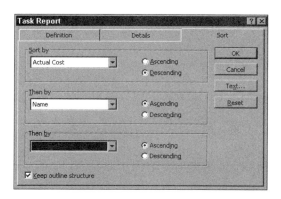

6. Select the Ascending or Descending radio button to organize your information numerically or alphabetically from lowest-to-highest or highest-to-lowest value.

7. (Optional) Repeat Steps 4 and 5 using the Then By text boxes to set a second and then a third criterion for sorting, if you want.

8. (Optional) If you want to keep the project outline structure relative to summary and subtasks, select the Keep Outline Structure check box.

9. Click OK to save the report settings.

Working Online with Microsoft Project

The Internet provides a powerful tool for enhancing communication among individuals who are working on a project. With Microsoft Project, e-mail is the tip of the communication iceberg. Project also offers features that let you notify resources about their assignments and let resources update you about their task activities and share documents online in Web-page format. In this part you find out how to insert hyperlinks in your projects and how to communicate with workgroups by e-mail and by using a new companion product for Microsoft Project 2000 called Project Central.

In this part . . .

Adding Hyperlinks

Hyperlinks are connections that enable you to jump to a document or a location on the World Wide Web. After you insert hyperlinks into tasks in Project, they appear as colored text in certain columns (Hyperlink Address, Hyperlink SubAddress, and Hyperlink Href) that you display in the Gantt Chart view. Whenever you click a hyperlink, you jump to the document, Web page, or e-mail address to which the hyperlink connects.

A hyperlink appears in one color before somebody follows the link to its destination and then changes to another color after someone follows the link.

In Project, you can insert one hyperlink in each task and multiple hyperlinks in each task's notes. To see hyperlinks, display the following hyperlink columns in any spreadsheet view:

✓ **Hyperlink Address:** Contains the address of a hyperlink

✓ **Hyperlink SubAddress:** Contains a location within a document, such as a task ID number in another Project file

✓ **Hyperlink Href:** Combines the combination of a Hyperlink Address and any Hyperlink SubAddress

To insert a hyperlink into a Project task, follow these steps:

1. Click the Gantt Chart icon in the View bar along the left side of the Project screen. The Gantt Chart view appears.

2. Select the task in which you want to insert the link.

3. Choose Insert↦Hyperlink. The Insert Hyperlink dialog box appears.

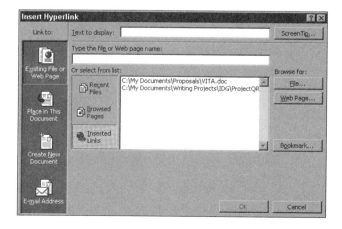

4. Click the Recent Files, Browsed Pages, or Inserted Links button to select the item to which you want to link or use the Browse For buttons (File, Web Page, or Bookmark) to locate the item.

5. After you find the document to which you want to link, click to select it.

6. Select the method for your link from the Link To view bar on the left side of the dialog box. You can choose to link to the following items: Existing File or Web Page, Place in This Document, Create a New Document, or E-mail Address.

7. Click OK to set the hyperlink.

Your task hyperlink is now available by displaying the column titled Indicator or any of the three hyperlink columns in the Gantt Chart view. To display these columns in any spreadsheet view, choose Insert⇨Column, select the column from the list, and click OK. After the column appears, click the link in the column to follow it.

Communicating with Workgroups

Staying in touch with the resources involved in your project is vital to your success. You need to communicate with resources about their assignments and the status of your project and to forward supporting documents to them for review. On the other side, they need to communicate with you about their activities. Project's robust workgroup features are married to the power of the Internet to offer you several ways to stay connected.

Displaying the Workgroup toolbar

In the Workgroup toolbar, you find many of the tools that enable you to communicate with your team. To display the Workgroup toolbar, choose View⇨Toolbars⇨Workgroup.

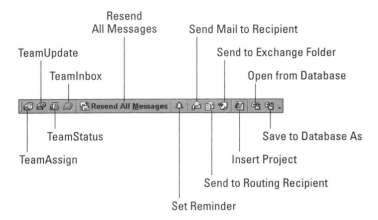

The Workgroup toolbar's first four tools (TeamAssign, TeamUpdate, TeamStatus, and TeamInbox) are used to send and receive assignments and updates for your resources by e-mail. The other tools perform the following functions:

✔ **Set Reminder** turns on a reminder in Microsoft Outlook for a task that you select.

✔ **Send Mail to Recipient** sends the open project file as an attachment to an e-mail message.

✔ **Send to Routing Recipient** opens a routing slip to send the open project file as an attachment to an e-mail message that you're sending to a list of recipients.

✔ **Send to Exchange Folder** saves the file in a Microsoft Exchange folder that you designate when prompted.

✔ **Insert Project** inserts another project into your project. The inserted project then appears as a task in your project.

✔ **Open from Database** lets you quickly open a file that was saved in Microsoft Access format. Access is Microsoft Office's database program; saving project data in a database format is a common practice for sharing that data with those who don't have Project installed.

✔ **Save to Database As** allows you to save the current project information in database format.

Sending assignments with TeamAssign

TeamAssign is a Microsoft Project feature that lets you send a message to one or more recipients to notify them of their task assignments. The message is sent by e-mail or Project Central, which is a companion product that integrates communication with team members. *See also* "Working with Project Central" later in this part. After a team member receives a TeamAssign message, that member can then reply to you and accept or decline the assignment. *See also* Part VII for detailed information about making assignments with TeamAssign.

Requesting updates with TeamStatus

With TeamStatus, you can send a message to resources requesting updates on the tasks to which they're assigned. A TeamStatus message lists the tasks to which resources are assigned, including the most current information about work hours, start and finish dates, and the amount of task work remaining and complete. The message requests that resources update the information and then return it to you.

To send a TeamStatus request, follow these steps:

1. Click the Gantt Chart icon in the View bar along the left side of the Project screen. The Gantt Chart view appears.

2. If you want to send the message for a single task, be sure you click to select that task in the Task Name column before proceeding.

3. Click the TeamStatus button on the Workgroup toolbar. The Workgroup Mail dialog box appears offering you the choice of sending a message about the single task or the entire project.

4. Click to select the Selected Task or Entire Project radio button and then click OK. The TeamStatus dialog box appears with a message already addressed to the appropriate resources for the selected task or the entire project, depending on the choice you make.

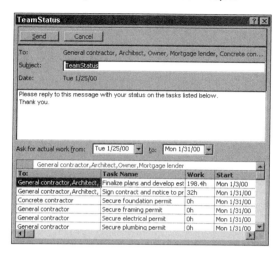

5. Use the default subject or type a different subject in the Subject text box.

6. In the middle of the dialog box, use the default message, modify it, or replace it.

7. In the Ask For Actual Work From text boxes, use the drop-down calendars to select a timeframe for the TeamStatus report.

8. After you complete any modifications, click Send to send the message.

Communicating assignment changes with TeamUpdate

TeamUpdate is an automated e-mail message that you send (after your team assignments are accepted) to notify resources of assignment changes.

To use TeamUpdate, follow these steps:

1. Click the Gantt Chart icon in the View bar along the left side of the Project screen. The Gantt Chart view appears.

2. If you want to update resource assignments on specific tasks, click to select the tasks in the Task Name column in the Gantt Chart view.

3. Click the TeamUpdate button on the Workgroup toolbar. The TeamUpdate dialog box appears.

4. Use the default subject or type a different subject in the Subject text box.

5. In the middle of the dialog box, use the default message, modify it, or replace it.

6. Click Send to send the update message to the assigned resources.

To select tasks that aren't adjacent in your schedule, hold down the CTRL key as you click the tasks.

Saving Files as Web Pages

You can easily communicate project information by saving a file as a Web page and then posting that page online for all to see. Microsoft Project includes Export Mapping, which uses a data map to determine what information to export to another format, such as a Web page.

To save a project as a Web page, follow these steps:

1. Choose File⇨Save As a Web Page from the menu bar. The Save As dialog box appears.

2. Type a name in the File Name field.

3. Click Save. The Export Mapping dialog box appears.

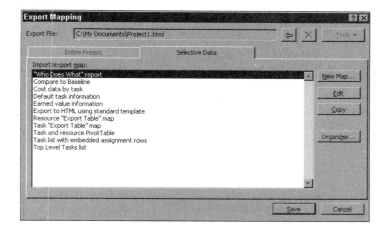

4. In the Import/Export Map field, click the Selective Data tab and then select an export map that provides the data you want to include.

5. Click Save to save the file as a Web page.

You can post the Web page to a site on your intranet or to a Web site. You can also post the Web page in an Exchange folder by using the Send To Exchange Folder button on the Workgroup toolbar so that you and your team can access it from that folder.

For information about editing import/export maps, take a look at *Microsoft Project 2000 Bible,* by Elaine Marmel (published by IDG Books Worldwide, Inc.).

Tracking Work with Microsoft Outlook

In Microsoft Project, you can use Project Central, a companion product, to work online with your resources through an intranet or Web site, or you can use an e-mail program, such as Microsoft Outlook, to do the same thing. If you use Microsoft Outlook to communicate with your team, Project includes the following features (that other e-mail programs don't offer) to save you time when tracking a project's work:

- ✔ Task assignments that a resource accepts are automatically added to that resource's Outlook to-do list.

- ✔ Time spent working with a project file can automatically be tracked in the Outlook Journal.

- ✔ Entries in the Outlook Address Book can be used to add resource information to a project.

Tracking in Outlook Journal

You can use the Outlook Journal to record the time you spend working on a Project file. This feature not only enables you to measure the time you spend managing a project, but it also enables Outlook to find project files based on any activity Outlook logs on to them.

To set up Outlook to track activity on Project files, follow these steps:

1. Open Outlook from the Windows desktop by choosing Start⇨Programs⇨Microsoft Outlook.

2. Choose Tools⇨Options from the menu bar. The Options dialog box appears.

3. Click the Preferences tab.

4. Click Journal Options. The Journal Options dialog box appears.

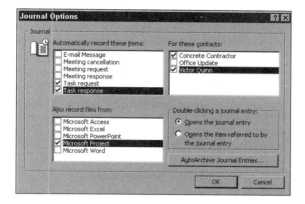

5. In the Automatically Record These Items and the For These Contacts fields respectively, select the items you want recorded and the resources you want them recorded for.

6. Click OK.

7. Click OK again to save the settings.

Note: Whether Outlook is open or not, activity is recorded when you or someone else works on a Project file.

Entering resources in Project with the Outlook Address Book

To automatically enter resource information in Project, you can use information that you previously entered in your Outlook contact database. That way, in addition to quickly creating resources, you can also copy information, such as e-mail addresses and group affiliations, from Outlook to Project.

To add a resource to a project by using the Outlook Address Book, follow these steps:

1. Click the Gantt Chart icon in the View bar along the left side of the Project screen. The Gantt Chart icon appears.

2. Click Assign Resources on the Standard toolbar. The Assign Resources dialog box appears.

3. Click the Address button. The Select Resources dialog box appears.

4. Click the name of the resource you want to add.

5. Click Add.

In Outlook, if you select a distribution list rather than a resource, you're asked whether you want to add the list as a single resource or to add each member as an individual resource in your project.

Working with Project Central

New to Project 2000 is a companion product called Microsoft Project Central. Project Central can be used as an alternative to an e-mail program to enable the flow of communication online among your workgroup members through either an intranet or a Web site.

Project Central provides a centralized format for viewing project information online and for communicating with your team. The Project Central interface lets you and your team members (who don't have access to Project) control data easily. If you configure Project to use Project Central, all TeamAssign, TeamStatus, and TeamUpdate messaging goes through Project Central, and information is organized in easy-to-use, graphically attractive Web pages.

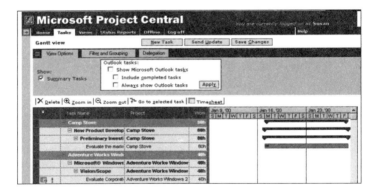

With Project Central, your team can see Project data without having Project installed. The project manager, however, must have Project. Project Central must be installed on a Web server that's accessible to your company intranet, and you must open an account for each project resource. After Project Central is installed, you and your team can reach Project Central by locating its URL with a Web browser, or in Project by choosing Tools⇔Workgroup⇔ TeamInbox. **See** the Appendix for information on installing Project Central.

Updating project data with Project Central

When resources respond to a TeamStatus message to update you on task information (such as start and finish dates or work completed), Project enables you to automatically update that information in your Project file by using Project Central.

To accept work updates in your project, follow these steps:

1. Choose Tools⊅Workgroup⊅TeamInbox. The Project Central home page appears.

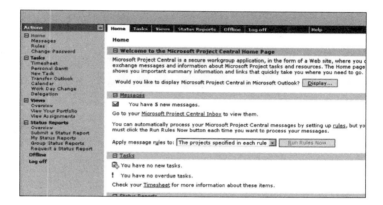

2. Click Messages to view any messages you receive.

3. Click a specific message and then click Open Message.

4. Click Update to update the associated project file automatically.

If you reply to a message before using the update feature, Project Central deletes the message you're responding to, making it no longer available to an automatic update.

Using Timesheet to track activity

Timesheet is a Project Central feature that enables resources to enter the amount of time they work on a project on a task-by-task basis. A message then goes to you as the project manager updating you on the project's status. You can then choose to have that data automatically update the project file or to make the updates manually.

To use Timesheet, have your resources follow these steps:

1. Choose Tools⇨Workgroup⇨TeamInbox from the menu bar. The Project Central home page appears.

2. Select Timesheet from the Actions list along the left side of the page.

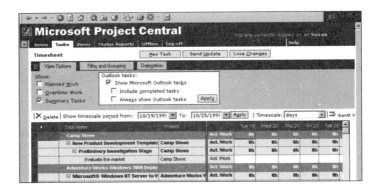

3. In the Task Name column, find the task for which you want to record work and click the task name.

4. Select timescale information for the task in the Show Timescale Period From and To drop-down lists.

5. Click a cell under the date in which you want to record activity and enter the number of hours worked on the selected task on that day.

6. After you finish recording task activity, click Send Update to send the information to the project manager.

For more about Project Central, see *Microsoft Project 2000 For Dummies,* by Martin Doucette, and *Microsoft Project 2000 Bible,* by Elaine Marmel (both published by IDG Books Worldwide, Inc.).

Installation Requirements for Project Central

Microsoft Project 2000 has a new companion product called Project Central, which is included on your Microsoft Project CD. Project Central — used instead of an e-mail program to communicate with your workgroup members — includes the following features:

- TeamAssign, TeamStatus, and TeamUpdate messages and responses

- Routed documents

- Special elements that allow resources to delegate assignments

- Web page versions of a project

- Timesheet, which enables your resources to track task time and you to perform automatic project updates

Project Central gives the project manager control over the information that people can access and uses Windows NT authentication to provide information security.

With Project Central, your team members also benefit by seeing Project files and having input to them, even without having Project installed on their computers. However, Project must be installed on the project manager's computer, and Project Central must be installed on a Web server that's accessible to all team members through a network. **See also** Part XIII for information about using Project Central's features.

Setting Up Project Central

Team members can access Project Central as soon as they have their accounts (which are set up automatically the first time they send a workgroup message to the project manager) and a browser. If anyone doesn't have a browser, installing the Microsoft Project Central Browser Module on the main Project installation screen is easy. Microsoft Project Central Server is also installed on your Web server from the main Project installation screen. *See* "Installing a Web Server" later in this appendix.

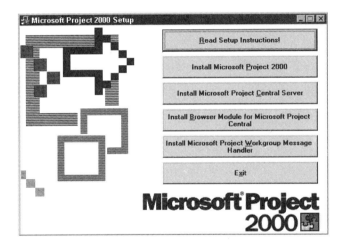

You can find more detailed information on installing Project Central in *Microsoft Project 2000 Bible*, by Elaine Marmel (published by IDG Books Worldwide, Inc.).

Before you can use Project Central, you must have the following setups:

✔ Microsoft Project installed on at least one person's computer, typically the project manager's.

✔ Microsoft Project Central Server installed on a server computer with Microsoft Windows NT Server 4.0 Service Pack 4 or later, or another server with Internet Information Server 4.0 or later.

✔ A Microsoft Project Central license for each member of your group. One license is included with Project.

✔ A Web browser for everyone accessing Project Central — such as Microsoft Internet Explorer 4.01 Service Pack 1 or later, or the Project Central Browser Module.

✔ Access to a network and a unique network identification, which is required so that Project Central can identify each team member's computer for routing communications.

Usually, your network administrator installs Project Central on your network and sets up accounts for all your project users, because setting some network permissions and security parameters may be required. To assist your IS staff, both Project and Project Central provide detailed documentation on installation requirements in their help systems. The Microsoft Project CD also includes a helpful document titled setupsvr.htm.

Installing a Web Server

If your server computer runs Windows NT Server 4.0 or later, you don't need to install a Web server at all, because this server software incorporates an active Web server called Internet Information Server (IIS). However, if you do need to install a Web server, use the Microsoft Personal Web Server that's located on the Project CD.

 If you do not use a Microsoft Web server, you have to download IIS from the Microsoft Web site. Also, you may have some configuration problems with other Web servers. The Microsoft Project CD contains a file, pjread8.txt, that addresses these problems.

Configuring Project Central

After installing Project Central and a Web server, you can set up your computer to use Project Central by following these steps:

1. From the Windows desktop, choose Start⇨Programs⇨Microsoft Project.

2. Choose Tools⇨Options. The Options dialog box appears.

3. Click the Workgroup tab.

4. Select Web from the Default Workgroup Messages For *the specific project name* drop-down list.

5. In the Microsoft Project Central Server URL text box, type the URL for accessing Project Central Server. The remaining fields in the dialog box are now accessible to you.

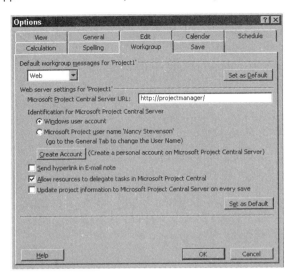

6. Choose whether you want to use your Windows User Account or Microsoft Project User Name (Project Central) authentication to identify you by selecting the appropriate radio button. Note: The Windows User Account does not require you to type a name and password when you access Project Central.

7. Set any preferences you want by placing a check in the following check boxes:

   • ***Send Hyperlink in E-mail Note:*** Each time a team member gets a Project Central message, it includes a hyperlink to Project Central.

   • ***Allow Resources to Delegate Tasks in Microsoft Project Central***: Resources can delegate tasks to others, with your approval.

   • Update Project Information to Microsoft Project Central Server on Every Save: Each time you save a file, you also automatically update Project Central Server.

8. Click Set As Default to save these settings for all your projects.

Before you can use Project Central, you need to have an account. Project Central sets up an account for you the first time you send a workgroup message.

If your server is set up to use Windows NT authentication, a logon screen appears when workgroup members first log on to Project Central. In the User Name drop-down list, workgroup members select their names. If a team member's name does not appear in the drop-down list, that team member can click Setting Up a Microsoft Project Central Account on the left side of the Web page to add his or her name. After the User Name has been entered, resources can type their passwords and then click Enter to access Project Central.

Glossary: Tech Talk

ACWP (actual cost of work performed): Cost of actual work performed to date on a project, plus any fixed costs.

ALAP (as late as possible): A constraint put on a task's timing (based on its dependency relationships) to make the task occur as late as possible in the project schedule. *See also* dependency.

ASAP (as soon as possible): A constraint put on a task's timing (based on its dependency relationships) to make the task occur as early as possible in the project schedule. *See also* dependency.

BAC (budget at completion): The total of all planned costs for completing a task. *See also* baseline costs.

BCWP (budgeted cost of work performed): Also called earned value, this term refers to the value of work completed. A task with $1,000 of associated costs has accrued a baseline value of $750 when 75 percent complete.

BCWS (budgeted cost of work scheduled): The planned completion percentage times the planned costs. This calculated value totals a task's completed work and its remaining planned costs.

CV (cost variance): The difference between the planned costs (baseline costs) and the combination of actual costs to date and estimated costs remaining (scheduled costs). The cost variance is either positive (over budget) or negative (under budget).

EAC (estimate at completion): The total scheduled cost for resource effort on a specific task. This calculation combines the costs incurred to date with costs estimated for a task's remaining work.

WBS (work breakdown structure): Automatically assigned numbers that reflect the outline structure for each project task. Government project reports often require WBS codes.

actual: The cost of the percentage of work that has been completed on a task.

base calendar: The default calendar on which all new tasks are based, unless a resource-specific calendar is applied. *See also* resource calendars.

baseline: The detailed project plan against which actual work is tracked.

baseline cost: The total planned costs for a project's tasks, before any actual costs are incurred.

calendar: The various settings for hours in a workday, days in a workweek, holidays, and non-working days on which a project schedule is based.

circular dependency: A timing relationship among tasks that creates an endless loop that cannot be resolved.

collapse: To close a project outline to hide subtasks from view.

combination view: A Project view with the task details appearing at the bottom of the screen.

constraint: A parameter that forces a task to fit a specific timing. For example, a task can be constrained to start as late as possible in a project.

cost: The amount linked to a project task when you assign resources, which are equipment, materials, or people with associated fees or hourly rates.

critical path: The series of tasks that must occur on time for the overall project to meet its deadline.

critical task: A task on the critical path. *See also* critical path.

cross tab: A report format that compares two intersecting sets of data; for example, you can generate a cross-tab report showing costs of critical tasks that are running late.

cumulative cost: The planned total cost to date for a resource on a particular task. This calculation adds the costs already incurred on a task to any planned costs remaining for the uncompleted portion of the task.

cumulative work: The planned total work of a resource on a particular task. This calculation adds the work completed on a task to any planned work remaining for the uncompleted portion of the task.

current date line: The vertical line in a Gantt chart indicating today's date and time. *See also* Gantt chart.

deadline date: A date you assign to a task that doesn't constrain the task's timing. However, if a deadline date is assigned, Project indicates whether that task finishes past its deadline.

demote: To move a task to a lower level of detail in the project's outline hierarchy.

dependency: A timing relationship between two tasks in a project. A dependency causes a task to occur before or after another task, or to begin or end at some point during the life of the other task.

detail task: *See* subtask.

duration: The amount of time it takes to complete a task.

duration variance: The difference between the planned (baseline) task duration and the current estimated task duration, based on activity to date and any remaining activity.

earned value: A reference to the value of work completed. A task with $1,000 of associated costs has a baseline value of $750 when 75 percent complete. *See also* BCWP.

effort driven: A task that takes an assigned amount of effort to complete. When you add resources to an effort-driven task, the assigned effort is distributed among the task resources.

estimated duration: A best guess of a task's duration. When you enter an estimated duration for a task, you can then apply a filter to display only tasks with estimated duration, which reflects the fact that they have questionable timing.

expand: To open a project outline to reveal both summary tasks and subtasks.

expected duration: An estimate of the actual duration of a task based on performance to date.

external task: A task in another project. You can set links between tasks in your project and external tasks.

finish date: The date on which a project or task is estimated to be or actually is completed.

finish-to-finish relationship: A dependency relationship in which one task must finish at the same time that another task finishes.

finish-to-start relationship: A dependency relationship in which one task must finish at the same time that another task starts.

fixed cost: A cost that doesn't increase or decrease based on the time a resource spends on a task. Consultants' fees or permit fees are examples of fixed costs.

fixed date: A certain date on which a task must occur. Dependency relationships will not cause fixed-date tasks to move earlier or later in the schedule. The last day of your company's fiscal year is an example of a fixed date.

fixed duration: A length of time required to complete a task, which remains constant no matter how many resources are assigned to the task. Travel time is an example of a fixed-duration task.

float: *See* slack.

Gantt chart: A standard project-management tracking device that displays task information alongside a chart that shows task timing in bar-chart format.

gap: *See* lag.

grouping: The organization of tasks by a customized field for the purpose of summarizing costs or other factors.

ID number: The number assigned to a task based on its sequence in the schedule.

lag: The amount of downtime between the end of one task and the beginning of another. Lag is built into a dependency relationship between tasks when you indicate that a certain amount of time must pass before the successor task can begin.

leveling: A calculation used by Project that modifies resource assignments to tasks for the purpose of resolving resource conflicts.

linking: 1) To establish a connection between two tasks in separate schedules so that task changes in the first schedule are reflected in the second. 2) To establish dependencies among project tasks.

material resources: The supplies or other items used to complete a task (one of two resource categories, the other being work resources).

milestone: A task of zero duration which marks a moment in time or an event in a schedule.

network diagram: An illustration that graphically represents workflow among a project's tasks, and one of Microsoft Project's standard views.

node: In the Network Diagram view, a box containing information about individual project tasks.

nonworking time: Time when a resource is not currently assigned to any task in a project.

outline: The structure of summary and subordinate tasks in a project.

overallocation: When a resource is assigned to spend more time than that resouce's work calendar permits, working on a single task or a combination of tasks that occur at the same time.

overtime: Any work scheduled beyond a resource's standard work hours; overtime work can carry a different rate than a resource's regular rate.

percent complete: The amount of work on a task that has already been accomplished, expressed as a percentage.

PERT chart: A standard project-management tracking form indicating workflow among project tasks. Called Network Diagram in the latest version of Project. *See also* network diagram.

predecessor: In a dependency relationship, the task designated to occur before another task. *See also* dependency and successor.

priorities: A ranking of importance that is assigned to tasks. When you use resource leveling to resolve project conflicts, priority is a factor in the leveling calculation. A higher priority task is less likely than a lower priority task to incur a delay during the leveling process. *See also* resource leveling.

progress lines: Gantt Chart bars that overlap the baseline taskbar and allow you to compare the baseline with a task's tracked progress.

project: A series of tasks that achieve a specific goal. A project seeks to meet the triple constraints of time, quality, and cost.

Project Central: A Web-based companion product of Microsoft Project that enables team members to enter information about their tasks into an overall project schedule without actually having Project installed on their own computers.

project management: The discipline that studies various methods, procedures, and concepts used to control the progress and outcome of projects.

promote: To move a task to a higher level in a project's outline hierarchy.

recurring task: A task that is repeated during the life of a project. Regular project team meetings or progress reviews are typical recurring tasks.

resource: A cost associated with a task, a resource is a person, a piece of equipment, materials, or a fee.

resource contouring: To change the time when a resource starts working on a task. You can use contouring to vary the amount of work a resource performs on a task over the life of that task.

resource driven: A task whose timing is determined by the number of resources assigned to it.

resource leveling: A process used to modify resource assignments to resolve resource conflicts.

resource pool: 1) A group of resources that are assigned as a group to an individual task (for example, a pool of administrative workers assigned to generate a report). 2) A group of resources created in a centralized location that multiple project managers can access and assign to their projects.

roll up: The calculation by which all subtask values are "rolled up" or summarized in a summary task.

slack: The time available to delay a task before the task becomes critical. Slack is used up when any delay in a task will delay the overall project deadline. Also called float.

split tasks: Tasks that have a break in their timing. When you split a task, you stop it midway and then start it again at a later time.

start date: The date on which a project begins.

start-to-finish relationship: A dependency relationship in which one task cannot start until another task finishes.

start-to-start relationship: A dependency relationship in which two tasks must start at the same time.

subproject: A copy of a second project inserted into a project. The inserted project becomes a phase of the project in which it is inserted.

subtask: A task detailing a specific step in a project. This detail is rolled up into a higher-level summary task. Also called a subordinate task. *See also* roll up.

successor: In a dependency relationship, a successor task begins after another task begins or ends. *See also* dependency.

summary task: In a project outline, a task that has subordinate tasks. A summary task rolls up the details of its subtasks and has no timing of its own. *See also* roll up.

task: An individual step performed to reach a project's goal.

template: A format in which a file can be saved; the template saves elements, such as calendar settings, formatting, and tasks. New project files can be based on a template to save time reestablishing saved settings.

timescale: The area of a Gantt Chart view that displays units of time and bars that, when placed against those units of time, graphically represent the timing of tasks.

tracking: To record the actual progress of work completed and the costs accrued on a project's tasks.

variable rate: A shift in resource cost that can be set to occur at specific times during a project. For example, if a resource is expected to receive a raise, or if equipment lease rates are scheduled to increase, you can assign variable rates for those resources.

workload: The amount of work any resource performs at any given time, taking into account all tasks to which the resource is assigned.

work resources: The people or equipment that perform work necessary to accomplish a task. *See also* material resources.

workspace: A set of files and project settings that you can save and reopen together, so that you pick up work where you stopped on a project or projects.

Index

Get it Done With Dummies
Bestsellers on Every Topic!

 TECHNOLOGY TITLES

INTERNET/ONLINE

America Online® For Dummies®, 5th Edition	John Kaufeld	0-7645-0502-5	$19.99 US/$27
Banking Online Dummies®	Paul Murphy	0-7645-0458-4	$24.99 US/$27
eBay™ For Dummies®	Roland Warner	0-7645-0582-3	$19.99 US/$27
E-Mail For Dummies®, 2nd Edition	John R. Levine, Carol Baroudi, & Arnold Reinhold	0-7645-0131-3	$24.99 US/$34
Genealogy Online For Dummies®	Matthew L. Helm & April Leah Helm	0-7645-0377-4	$24.99 US/$34
Internet Auctions For Dummies®	Greg Holden	0-7645-0578-9	$24.99 US/$34
Internet Directory For Dummies®, 3ED Edition	Brad Hill	0-7645-0558-2	$24.99 US/$34
Internet Explorer 5 for Windows® For Dummies®	Doug Lowe	0-7645-0455-X	$19.99 US/$28
Investing Online For Dummies®, 2nd Edition	Kathleen Sindell, Ph.D.	0-7645-0509-2	$24.99 US/$34
Job Searching Online For Dummies®, 2nd Edition	Pam Dixon	0-7645-0673-0	$24.99 US/$34
Travel Planning Online For Dummies® 2nd Edition	Noah Vadnai	0-7645-0438-X	$24.99 US/$34
World Wide Web Searching For Dummies®, 2nd Ed.	Brad Hill	0-7645-0264-6	$24.99 US/$34
Yahoo!® For Dummies®	Brad Hill	0-7645-0582-3	$19.99 US/$27

OPERATING SYSTEMS

DOS For Dummies®, 3rd Edition	Dan Gookin	0-7645-0361-8	$19.99 US/$27
GNOME For Linux® For Dummies®	David D. Busch	0-7645-0650-1	$24.99 US/$37
LINUX® For Dummies®, 2nd Edition	John Hall, Craig Witherspoon, & Coletta Witherspoon	0-7645-0421-5	$24.99 US/$34
Mac® OS 8.5 For Dummies®	Bob LeVitus	0-7645-0397-9	$19.99 US/$28
Red Hat® Linux® For Dummies®	Jon "maddog" Hall	0-7645-0663-3	$24.99 US/$37
Small Business Windows® 98 For Dummies®	Stephen Nelson	0-7645-0425-8	$24.99 US/$34
UNIX® For Dummies®, 4th Edition	John R. Levine & Margaret Levine Young	0-7645-0419-3	$19.99 US/$27
Windows® 95 For Dummies®, 2nd Edition	Andy Rathbone	0-7645-0180-1	$19.99 US/$27
Windows® 98 For Dummies®	Andy Rathbone	0-7645-0261-1	$19.99 US/$27
Windows® 2000 Professional For Dummies®	Andy Rathbone	0-7645-0641-2	$19.99 US/$29
Windows® 2000 Server For Dummies®	Ed Tittel	0-7645-0341-3	$24.99 US/$37

WEB DESIGN & PUBLISHING

Active Server™ Pages For Dummies®, 2nd Edition	Bill Hatfield	0-7645-0603-X	$24.99 US/$37
Cold Fusion 4 For Dummies®	Alexis Gutzman	0-7645-0604-8	$24.99 US/$37
Creating Web Pages For Dummies®, 4th Edition	Bud Smith & Arthur Bebak	0-7645-0504-1	$24.99 US/$34
Dreamweaver™ For Dummies®	Janine Warner	0-7645-0407-X	$24.99 US/$35
FrontPage® 2000 For Dummies®	Asha Dornfest	0-7645-0423-1	$24.99 US/$34
HTML 4 For Dummies®, 2nd Edition	Ed Tittel & Stephen Nelson James	0-7645-0572-6	$24.99 US/$34
Java™ For Dummies®, 2nd Edition	Aaron E. Walsh	0-7645-0140-2	$24.99 US/$34
PageMill™ 2 For Dummies®	Deke McClelland & John San Filippo	0-7645-0028-7	$24.99 US/$34
XML™ For Dummies®, 2nd Edition	Ed Tittel	0-7645-0692-7	$24.99 US/$34

DESKTOP PUBLISHING GRAPHICS/MULTIMEDIA

Adobe® InDesign™ For Dummies®	Deke McClelland	0-7645-0599-8	$19.99 US/$27
CorelDRAW™ 9 For Dummies®	Deke McClelland	0-7645-0523-8	$19.99 US/$27
Desktop Publishing and Design For Dummies®	Roger C. Parker	1-56884-234-1	$19.99 US/$27
Digital Photography For Dummies®, 3rd Edition	Julie Adair King	0-7645-0646-3	$24.99 US/$37
Microsoft® Publisher 98 For Dummies®	Jim McCarter	0-7645-0395-2	$19.99 US/$27
Visio 2000 For Dummies®	Debbie Walkowski	0-7645-0635-8	$19.99 US/$29

MACINTOSH

Macs® For Dummies®, 6th Edition	David Pogue	0-7645-0398-7	$19.99 US/$27
Macs® For Teachers™, 3rd Edition	Michelle Robinette	0-7645-0226-3	$24.99 US/$34
The iBook™ For Dummies®	David Pogue	0-7645-0647-1	$19.99 US/$29
The iMac For Dummies®, 2nd Edition	David Pogue	0-7645-0648-X	$19.99 US/$27

PC/GENERAL COMPUTING

Building A PC For Dummies®, 2nd Edition	Mark Chambers	0-7645-0571-8	$24.99 US/$34
Buying a Computer For Dummies®	Dan Gookin	0-7645-0313-8	$19.99 US/$27
Family Tree Maker For Dummies®	Matthew & April Helm	0-7645-0661-7	$19.99 US/$27
Illustrated Computer Dictionary For Dummies®, 3rd Edition	Dan Gookin & Sandra Hardin Gookin	0-7645-0143-7	$19.99 US/$27
Palm Computing® For Dummies®	Bill Dyszel	0-7645-0581-5	$24.99 US/$34
PCs For Dummies®, 7th Edition	Dan Gookin	0-7645-0594-7	$19.99 US/$27
QuickBooks 2000 For Dummies®	Stephen Nelson	0-7645-0665-X	$19.99 US/$29
Small Business Computing For Dummies®	Brian Underdahl	0-7645-0287-5	$24.99 US/$34
Smart Homes For Dummies®	Danny Briere	0-7645-0527-0	$19.99 US/$27
Upgrading & Fixing PCs For Dummies®, 4th Edition	Andy Rathbone	0-7645-0418-5	$19.99 US/$27

Get it Done With Dummies
Bestsellers on Every Topic!

 ## TECHNOLOGY TITLES

IDG BOOKS WORLDWIDE BOOK REGISTRATION

Register
This Book
and Win!

We want to hear from you!

Visit **http://my2cents.dummies.com** to register this book and tell us how you liked it!

- ✓ Get entered in our monthly prize giveaway.

- ✓ Give us feedback about this book — tell us what you like best, what you like least, or maybe what you'd like to ask the author and us to change!

- ✓ Let us know any other *For Dummies*® topics that interest you.

Your feedback helps us determine what books to publish, tells us what coverage to add as we revise our books, and lets us know whether we're meeting your needs as a *For Dummies* reader. You're our most valuable resource, and what you have to say is important to us!

Not on the Web yet? It's easy to get started with *Dummies 101*®: *The Internet For Windows*® *98* or *The Internet For Dummies*®3 at local retailers everywhere.

Or let us know what you think by sending us a letter at the following address:

For Dummies Book Registration
Dummies Press
10475 Crosspoint Blvd.
Indianapolis, IN 46256

™

BESTSELLING
BOOK SERIES